# Hand$_{in}$ Hand
## with Tommy

# Hand in Hand with Tommy
## A Testimony, 1939–1945

### by Mother: *HILDE HUPPERT*

Translated from the Hebrew by:
*YAEL CHAVER* and *REUVEN MORGAN*

**WITH**

# A Toast for Bertha
## A Short Novel

### by Son: *SHMUEL THOMAS HUPPERT*

Translated from the Hebrew by:
*REUVEN MORGAN*

gefen כפן
publishing house בית הוצאה לאור
JERUSALEM ♦ NEW YORK

*Hand in Hand with Tommy* and "A Toast for Bertha" appeared originally
in Hebrew, published by Moreshet and Sifryat Poalim, Tel Aviv.

Typesetting: Raphaël Freeman, Jerusalem Typesetting
Cover Design: Studio Paz, Jerusalem

ISBN 965-229-325-3

1   3   5   7   9   8   6   4   2

Gefen Publishing House
6 Hatzvi Street, Jerusalem 94386, Israel
972-2-538-0247
orders@gefenpublishing.com

Gefen Books
600 Broadway, Lynbrook, NY 11563, USA
1-800-477-5257
orders@gefenpublishing.com

**www.israelbooks.com**

Printed in Israel

*Send for our free catalogue*

# CONTENTS

# FOREWORD

*T*HE ELDERLY GENTLEMAN, now going slightly bald, who sits down to write the saga of a manuscript written by his mother, Hilde Huppert, is the same wavy-haired child who can be seen seated on his mother's knee in the photograph at the front of this book. A seemingly idyllic snapshot, it was taken in May 1942 in the little Polish village of Ivonitch, some six months before we were arrested and imprisoned in Krosno. From there we were transferred to the ghetto in Rzeszow, then sent to the central prison in Cracow, and finally to the Bergen-Belsen concentration camp.

The fact that my mother never let go of my hand during the entire period of the Holocaust and that my father, who was on a tourist visa in Palestine, succeeded in sending us immigration certificates has always seemed to me to be a miracle.

WHEN MOTHER AND I FINALLY arrived at the Promised Land in July 1945 she began to relate the details of what the Germans had done to the Jews to anyone who cared to listen. Our friends and relatives were shocked to hear the horror stories she would tell about the ghetto and Bergen-Belsen. They would sit by her side, hold her hand, and weep. Some felt guilty because my mother's piercing glance seemed to challenge them with the question: *Why didn't you try harder to save your own families?*

After a couple of months in Palestine we had fewer and fewer visitors to our one-room apartment. Those who still came tried to persuade Mama to forget the past, to start a new life. It was hard for her to accept such advice: she still dreamt of her murdered mother and sisters. She would wake up screaming in the night and suffer from chronic stomach pains. When she found little relief from the doctors, who recommended tranquilizers along with rest and relaxation, it was my father who had the idea: "Why not try writing your memoirs? Maybe that will free you from your nightmares?"

Mama was hesitant. She had never seen herself as a writer. But the moment she took hold of a fountain pen, the visions of the past wrote themselves – and in German.

I can recall her sitting at the folding table by the window that overlooked the Haifa bay, writing and weeping. She was reliving the agonies of abandoning her mother and her little niece, Ruthy; the fearful nights in the Monte Lupe prison in Cracow; and the months of starvation and cold on the bunks of Bergen-Belsen.

When she finished her writing on October 20, 1945, she felt exhausted and completely drained. She read the manuscript with astonishment, amazed that Hilde Huppert from the Biegeleisen family, who had only completed elementary school (but with perfect grades), had actually written a book. She then added the title: *Warum ist uns das geschehen?* – Why should this have happened to us?

A FRIEND OF THE FAMILY suggested showing the manuscript to the well-known author Arnold Zweig, who lived in Haifa at that time. Zweig, who was elderly and already half blind, asked my mother to read the manuscript to him, which she eagerly did. Later, Mama described to me how Zweig listened closely, often shaking his head as if in disbelief and mumbling to himself, "Is this the Germany I knew? The Germany of Goethe and Schiller?"

A contract was drawn up and both he and my mother set out to work. Zweig took upon himself the task of editing the text, and on his return to East Germany (where he was appointed as the president of the Academy of Arts), he arranged for the book to be published in both Czech and German. He seemed to be so enamored of the work that he published it under his own name, with an acknowledgement in the preface that read, "The following pages are not my own, they were handed to me by their author, Frau Hilde Huppert, to be prepared for publication."

Zweig gave the German edition a title with mythological connotations: *Fahrt Zum Acheron – A Journey to the River Styx* – a name Mother had rejected as they worked together on editing the manuscript. She would have preferred something more concrete.

I am fully aware that in recalling this incident I may be prejudiced. It might well be that Arnold Zweig used his own name in order to ensure that the book reach a wider public. The first editions, published both in Czechoslovakia and in East Germany, were censored. For example, the fact that our transport was actually liberated by American troopers was omitted. It is clear from both his prologue and epilogue that Zweig was doing the best to toe the Communist Party line.

Hebrew-language publishers received the German manuscript in the late 1940s. It took them several months to read it and then return it with notes of apology. They claimed that it was too soon to publish a book about the Holocaust. They promised Mama that her book would eventually see the light of day and recommended that she be patient and keep it in the drawer. I can readily imagine the resentment of both Mama and of Arnold Zweig on reading these polite rejection slips. Zweig's own reactions were later detailed in his correspondence with Lion Feuchtwanger.

FOR MANY YEARS I served as head of the literary department of the Israeli Radio. In 1977, to mark our Holocaust Martyrs and Heroes Day, I broadcast an interview with my mother. I gave it the title "Mama Gave Me Birth Twice." Mother spoke so calmly and objectively that many listeners who would normally switch off when confronted with a program about the Holocaust kept listening and were extremely moved. I received hundreds of responses, both written and verbal. People were begging to know more and to express their sympathy and admiration.

One of the listeners who contacted me was the poet and former partisan Abba Kovner, who asked what had become of the manuscript, which I had mentioned in the program. I still had a Hebrew translation that I had prepared as a birthday present for Mama in 1955. It was entitled *The Slaughterer Slaughtered*. On rereading it I could see that my passionate prose of that time and virulent title (taken from Bialik's poem on the Kishinev pogrom) were unsuited to the reading public of the seventies. So I went back to the original version and made another translation in a more factual and restrained style. This Hebrew version was approved by my mother, as was my title, *Hand in Hand with Tommy*.

*Hand in Hand with Tommy* was published by Moreshet, the publishing house named after Warsaw ghetto fighter Mordechai Anielevich, together with Sifryat Hapoalim in 1978. The book has appeared in eight editions.

This version has been published in Holland and in Germany, and in Israel in an Arabic translation. It was also submitted to various publishers in England and the United States whose reactions were positive, but fearful that it would be hard to sell. I refrained from showing their rejection slips to my aging mother.

In the meantime she had written two novels describing the ventures of Jewish and Polish underground warriors, one of which entitled *Doctor Veronika*, had been published in Holland and in

Poland. Mama was hoping that the appearance of *Hand in Hand with Tommy* might encourage an American publisher (or perhaps even a film producer) to show an interest in her additional writing.

IN HER PREFACE, written in 1946, my mother wrote that only by knowing the facts, future generations might be spared another Holocaust. Today, more than half a century after the end of World War Two, Neo-Nazis can be seen parading through the cities of Germany, beating up Asian immigrants, torching the hostels of migrant workers, and desecrating Jewish graveyards. Anti-Semitism threatens the Jews of Russia and even raises its ugly head in the more civilized countries of Western Europe and America. So-called scholars publish "research" in which they claim to "prove" that Hitler and the Nazis had no grand design for the Final Solution and that there was no systematic slaughter of six million Jews. They present the terrifying history, which we ourselves lived through (did Grandma Bluma, Grandpa Sigmund, Mama's three sisters, their husbands, and children simply "vanish"?), as a fiction, to be read with a certain interest and ultimately denied.

Not long ago a Swiss friend of the family was on a train from Vienna to Zurich when a well-dressed man in his seventies, who was seated next to her, opened up a conversation. He told her that he was a university professor specializing in the history of the Holocaust, "which was of course a fabrication of the Jews." At first she thought he must be joking.

"But surely everyone knows that the Nazis destroyed six million," she protested.

"I am amazed that an educated woman like you should believe such malicious slander," he reproved her. "Had you ever heard me lecture on the subject, you would understand there is no question of millions. Maybe a few hundred thousand. Most of the Jews were annihilated by the barbaric bombing raids the Americans inflicted on German cities."

"And Auschwitz?" she insisted. "There are documents and testimonies that the Germans slaughtered millions of Jews there. I've seen the photographs of the gas chambers."

"Those gas chambers," he informed her, "were fabricated after the war was over in order to substantiate the hate propaganda against the German people. And documents? Mere forgeries created by the news media, which we well know are totally controlled and financed by the Jews."

He seemed surprised when our friend rose abruptly and moved to another compartment.

It is also due to the existence of these so-called "professors" who attempt to rewrite history that the survivors must continue to bear witness. As time goes by, eyewitnesses are becoming fewer and fewer, but those still living owe this debt to their dead.

*HAND IN HAND WITH TOMMY* now reaches the American reader after a delay of fifty years. But it seems to me that after many recent publications by survivors, after millions of viewers watched the television mini-series *Holocaust,* after Spielberg's *Schindler's List,* and after the U.S. Holocaust Memorial Museum has been opened in Washington D.C., there is probably a place in the hearts of many readers for my mother's personal testimony.

When I asked my ninety-three-year-old mother if there was anything specific she wanted to convey to the American reading public, she replied: "Tell them I shall never forget those four American G.I.s who liberated us from the Germans. One of them was black; another wore the Star of David on a chain around his neck. I can still recall their amazed faces in that dusty Jeep and the U.S. army symbol. I remember kissing one of them, and I want the American people to know that I am grateful to them."

I WOULD LIKE to dedicate the book to my cousin, and my friend, Ruthy Hauben, whom I left in the Rzeszow Ghetto. Ruthy was murdered at the age of eight.

*Dr. Shmuel Tommy Huppert*
*Jerusalem, November 2003*

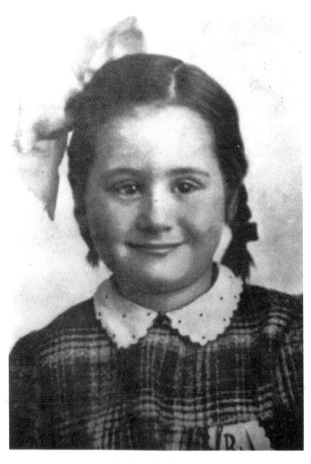

*Ruthy Hauben.*

# Hand<sub>in</sub> Hand
## with Tommy

**by Mother: *HILDE HUPPERT***

# Chapter 1
## WAR BEGINS

I WAS BORN INTO a traditional Jewish home in the town of Bielitz, Poland. My parents, Bluma and Zelig Biegeleisen, owned two shops and a stall that sold fruits and candies. My sisters and I worked in the shops, and our two brothers studied the Bible in a cheder and learned a trade. The regular customers used to talk of the "Beautiful Biegeleisen Girls," and the young men nicknamed our home "House of the Four Maidens." We made sure that Papa Zelig shouldn't hear any of this chatter.

Papa, short and stocky with a bushy beard, demanded that we conduct ourselves in all modesty and observe the commandments of the Jewish law. He used to lock my brother David in his room to make certain that he didn't play soccer on the Sabbath, but David would outwit him and slide down a rope from the second floor to join his pals. When Papa would discover that his son was missing, he would go on the rampage. Mama would try to calm him, begging him not to beat the boy.

"You keep out of this." (Papa would insist on keeping his voice down so as not to desecrate the Sabbath calm.) "But when he gets back, send him to me."

When at least three stars could be seen in the night sky, Papa took David into his room and closed the door. We could hear Papa yelling at him. David was stubborn and never uttered a sound.

Later, David joined the left-wing Zionist youth movement, Hashomer Hatzair, and immigrated to Palestine in 1929. We, the daughters, attended the German school in Bielitz, which had a gymnastics group into which the teacher was eager to recruit me. On asking my parents permission I met with a flat no from Papa. Mama, on the other hand, urgently pleaded that since I was small in stature, the physical exercise might help me develop. After a while Papa muttered, "So, let her try."

Unfortunately for me, Papa overheard one of our customers praising my appearance at a performance at school; one mention of my shapely legs was enough for him.

"What did I tell you, Bluma?" He chuckled, rubbing his beard with his strong thumb.

And that was the end of my career as a gymnast.

When I finished primary school the principal told my parents that as an outstanding pupil I should be sent to high school. Papa expressed gratitude for the compliments and scholarly advice, but voiced his firm opinion that his daughter had now acquired more than enough knowledge and that the time had come for her to learn a trade.

I trained as a seamstress for two years, after which I began to earn money sewing lingerie and embroidering. In the evenings I worked behind the counter in our shops, and on Sundays I worked at the stall Papa put up for the vacationers in the hills, near Bielitz. Papa Zelig would make his rounds of the shops, making sure that his daughters did not become too familiar with the clients.

Today, as I write about all this so many years later, I have the feeling I should treat Papa more fairly. I can recall him during the First World War, dragging a small cart laden with a huge cauldron of soup through the snow and the mud uphill to the hospital. Papa and Mama saw to it that the Jewish wounded soldiers would be able to eat hot kosher meals.

And another memory: my brother telling me that once, as he was walking along the street with Papa, some Polish drunkard spat out at them *"psha krew!"* (dog's blood). Papa stopped in his tracks, slapped the drunkard's face, and continued on his way.

Papa was a Zionist. He went to Palestine in 1925, prayed at the Western Wall, toured the Jewish colonies, and even purchased a plot of land close to Hebron. At the same time he was also tricked into buying (at a bargain price!) extensive acreage somewhere, not far from Tel Aviv, which turned to be a part of the Mediterranean Sea.

On returning to Bielitz, Papa was very eager to immigrate to the Holy Land, but Mama, concerned for the well-being of the children and claiming that Palestine had too hot a climate, persuaded him to postpone the journey year after year.

IT WAS A FOREGONE CONCLUSION that Papa (after consulting Mama) would be the one to select our future husbands. The prospective bridegroom (he would intone) must be a decent man, an upholder of the faith. Having already danced at the weddings of my three elder sisters, my turn finally came around. I had met Walter by chance at the home of one of our aunts in Teschen, a small Czechoslovakian-Silesian town not far from Bielitz. We had chatted a bit, both shyly and politely as befit distant relatives, with the aunt close by keeping both eyes and ears open. It was love at first sight.

After that first meeting, Walter developed a habit of coming "by chance" to Bielitz. He would visit our home and hold long conversations with Papa, whose keen eye soon discerned what drew the young man to visit. Summoning me to his room, he quizzed me about my feelings for the young Walter Huppert. I mustered all my courage and said: "I'm in love with Walter and I'd like to ask your permission to marry him."

I waited for the outburst, expecting an impassioned sermon about the sanctity of faith, but Papa replied mildly, "You are aware that the Hupperts are assimilated Jews."

"Yes, but Walter is a decent man."

"True, Hilde, true. But even were I to agree, his parents would never permit it. They are a wealthy family and Walter is their only son. I'm certain they will find him a rich and educated bride."

"But if they do agree, Papa, will you give your consent?"

"We'll discuss this later. I have to talk with your Mama. As for you, don't do anything foolish."

I know nothing of Walter's quarrels with his parents, but I assume that the Huppert family was forced to give in when it became clear that their obedient son was for once digging in his heels.

When I took leave of my parents, instead of lecturing me about keeping a strictly traditional home, Papa merely said to me: "In the Huppert family you won't be able to observe all the Jewish commandments. No, don't promise me that you will, that's a promise you'll never be able to keep. But be modest, and generous. Don't adopt the manners of the rich who look in the mirror and only see themselves; a generous person looks out of the window and sees others."

Whereas Mama whispered to me, "I'm so happy you won't have to shave your head and wear a wig, which is what they did to me. I do so love those long braids of yours."

Walter and I were married in 1935, and I moved to Teschen. My son, who was born a year later, was given his name by my father-in-law, Sigmund. Sigmund, a devoted Czech patriot, gave the child the name of the president of the Republic of Czechoslovakia, Thomas Masaryk. We called the boy Tommy. In those days we had no need to use his Hebrew name, Shmuel, which had only been given to appease my father.

OUR JOY did not last long. Relations between the Poles and the Czechs began to deteriorate, and we found ourselves caught in the midst of a conflict between the two nations. Polish demands to annex the Olsa River region were supported by the Third Reich, so that one morning we awoke to the sound of a military band and the echoing tramp of Polish troops. Teschen and the Olsa region had been handed over without a fight.

When the Poles came to Teschen we had our first taste of anti-Semitism, which had been a rare phenomenon among the Czechs. Jewish merchants were summoned to the Polish police and closely questioned about their connections with other Jews. Polish students picketed Jewish shops brandishing anti-Semitic placards and shouting insults at customers who dared try to make their way in.

In the spring of 1939 the family reached a decision that my husband should go to Palestine as a tourist and that I should remain in Teschen to look after Tommy and help my in-laws in their shops. Parting at the railway station I felt a grave sense of foreboding. Walter embraced me in his long arms, and I held back my tears. I felt ashamed to reveal such womanly weakness before my father-in-law, who seemed to be regarding us with a stern eye.

"What's all the fuss about?" he demanded. "Walter's only going to be away for a few months."

I let my husband go and took Tommy out of the hands of his nursemaid. The child stood silently, blowing a polite kiss toward Walter, who was already boarding the train. As it started to pull away, my father-in-law was waving his walking stick in a strict rhythm, my mother-in-law was waving a snow-white handkerchief. Suddenly I could see Putzi, Walter's pet dog, racing alongside the train. Eventually he came back exhausted, his tail between his legs.

We went back to running our large men's outfitters, but it was becoming difficult to obtain good merchandise and Sigmund had a hard time maintaining his previous standards. From time to time we would have *Volksdeutsche* or Polish customers who would select fine hosiery and linens and elegant suits, demanding credit for large sums. Sigmund, who had always insisted on cash purchases, now agreed to their arrogant demands.

"Credit for the gentleman, Valli." His calm remark concealed anxiety and a coming to terms with reality.

Some Czech acquaintances who had returned from a trip to Poland told us that they had heard rumors that a German army was encamped close to the Polish border. Polish officials, who dropped in to "buy" overcoats for a "journey" tried to reassure Sigmund, but he was constantly worried by what he read in the papers. One of our German salesgirls showed me a letter from her German fiancé dated August 22, 1939. It read, "We shall soon be together, have no fears. Our troops will take Silesia without firing a shot."

We held a family conference: It seemed best to leave Teschen for a while, so we started to pack our bags. Sigmund, Valli, and Tommy were to go to Ivonitch, a spa in Poland (near Krosno), where my father-in-law had once been cured. If war did indeed break out, I would follow with my widowed aunt Jenny, who was living with us. In the meantime, I was charged with looking after the house and the two shops.

ON THE NIGHT of September 1, the Polish constabulary quit the Olsa region, and the following morning the Germans took over Teschen. The local Germans, a considerable proportion of Teschen's population, welcomed these new conquerors with open arms.

A neighbor of ours who had managed to hide his car offered Aunt Jenny and me a lift in the direction of Bielitz. I dressed warmly, wore a raincoat, and shouldered a small knapsack we once used on hikes through the Beskeed hills.

"Hurry up, Hilde! We've got to get going!" My neighbor called from down below.

I took a last look around the room, at the curtains I had sewn myself, at the double bed, at my reflection in the mirror, and I was out, down the broad wooden staircase to the front door. I locked up the house and buried the keys deep inside my knapsack.

"Get into the car," my aunt urged, "and don't look back."

I did as I was told, but couldn't resist a last glance over my shoulder as the house receded, getting smaller and smaller all the time. A sharp turn, and it was gone.

THERE WERE SEVERAL other people we knew jammed into the car. Our neighbor was driving slowly, maneuvering his way between the files of refugees and military patrols at the roadside. At one of the checkpoints we were ordered out of the car to show our documents.

"Jewish gentlemen riding in a limousine!" jeered the sergeant. "Now take your bundles and get going on foot before I arrest all of you. And leave the suitcases in the car, you won't be able to haul them anyway."

We took leave of one another: Our friends had decided to go back home to Teschen, while Aunt Jenny and I set off on foot for Bielitz. Somewhere along the way the driver of a small car, upon being told we were the wives of Polish officers fighting at the front, was good enough to give us a lift.

By late afternoon we arrived at Mama Bluma's house. My father had died a year earlier. As we hugged each other I could feel her warmth overwhelming me and I burst into tears. She did too, but only for a moment. Soon Mama was wiping away her tears and bustling into the kitchen. While we ate she said, "Not to worry, Hildeleh, the Lord will protect us. Zelig, up in heaven, prays for us all the time."

Being anxious to get to Tommy, I didn't stay very long with Mama. A friend of my brother, whose car had not yet been impounded, took me as far as Cracow, where I hoped to find my sister Rega and a sister-in-law.

WE REACHED a darkened Cracow in the evening. Air-raid sirens were wailing and the streets were deserted. As we passed the train station, there was a vast explosion; after the shock, we could see smoke and flames towering above warehouses.

We quickly thanked the driver and hurried to my sister-in-law's apartment in the center of town. A knock on the door: no answer. A second, louder knocking brought out an old woman peering through a chink in the door from the neighboring apartment, muttering, "Not here. Down in the basement."

"Let's go down."

"I'm exhausted, Hilde." whispered Aunt Jenny. "I'll just wait here on the stairs."

"You're coming down with me!"

This was no time for giving in. So I dragged her and Jenny followed. Down below my sister-in-law greeted us: "I've got several guests already, but of course we can find room for you."

When the all-clear signal finally sounded she led some twenty men, women, and children upstairs to her apartment – a long silent line of refugees who had fled their homes and found a temporary haven.

The frequent alerts and consequent rush from the fourth floor to the basement were wearing me out. Now it was my turn to propose to Jenny that we remain in the apartment, despite the danger.

"You've got a son, Hilde!" she scolded me. "Come on, I'll help you down."

A few days later I moved in with my sister Rega, who had also found refuge in Cracow.

Cracow's streets were crowded with refugees from the regions captured by the Germans. The front was drawing nearer day by day;

thousands were trying to flee the city. Then came the announcement on the radio: All males to move eastward, and no further details. We women felt confused and helpless.

On a certain Wednesday I witnessed an already familiar parade, this time huge masses of Wehrmacht troops followed by units of the S.S. and Gestapo. The Wehrmacht continued on its road to conquest, but the S.S. and the Gestapo stayed on in Cracow. Their first actions were the proclamation of a curfew and street-arrests of Jews. Then came the raids on Jewish homes, the confiscation of valuables, and the detention of anyone who dared to protest.

From now on, day-to-day Jewish life was to be dictated by the Judenrat, the Jewish councils appointed by the German conquerors. The Judenrat was ordered to raise huge sums of money and to enlist a vast labor force. The money was handed over on time, and the men turned up punctually at the Judenrat offices. Many who set off for work never returned.

Only a few days after the invasion, rioters looted many of the ancient synagogues of Cracow. Once that job was done, the Germans set the synagogues ablaze.

Daily edicts were issued by the Nazi authorities on the radio and in the press: Jews were evicted from their homes in the more well-to-do suburbs and moved into poorer neighborhoods; Jewish property held abroad was subject to registration; each Jew was permitted to hold only two thousand zloty, the rest of his cash was to be "deposited" in specific banks. Anyone caught holding foreign currency faced the death penalty.

After a few weeks devoted to organizing themselves, the Nazis then issued an edict ordering all the Jews to wear an identifying badge, a white armband ten centimeters wide bearing a blue Star of David. This made things tricky for all of us. We were now instantly identifiable on the streets; we were refused service in the shops; and so we had to buy from the peasant farmers and the black market. In this way we were able to obtain small amounts of potatoes, flour, and eggs, by bartering valuable household goods. The Polish peasant enjoyed a profitable deal, and with a whetted appetite, the prices rocketed.

Generally speaking, it is fair to say that the Polish population, as a whole, was quite content with the attitude of the Germans toward the Jews. Many served as informers and eager guides, leading the Nazis to hidden caches of Jewish property. With the help of the Poles, the Gestapo was soon able to find its way around a vast city and locate the warehouses of Jewish businessmen and homes of the wealthy. Quite often, when I dared walk the streets without my armband, I would run into Poles openly gloating over tribulations of Jews. True, there were some exceptions, but these were few and far between.

At that time we began to hear rumors about what was going on in other towns in Poland: that six hundred Jews had been taken from Przemysl, ordered to dig their own graves and strip naked, and were then shot by the S.S.; that three hundred from Brzozow had been eliminated in the same manner; and that the Jews in Mielce had been ordered into the synagogue, after which the doors were locked from the outside and the building set afire.

After a long period of anxious waiting I finally got the good news that my family was still alive and well in Ivonitch. Bidding farewell to my sister, Aunt Jenny and I took off on foot to Krosno, concealing our incriminating armbands. A German driver of an army supply truck gave us a lift almostt all the way. He was friendly and cheerful, and apologized for not being able to have some fun with us, but explained that he had to be on time at the local Gestapo headquarters. From Krosno to the tiny holiday resort of Ivonitch there was a three-hour walk. When we got there we found Sigmund, Valli, and Tommy waiting for us. There was only one thing that shed a cloud on the joy of our reunion: my mother-in-law, Valli, was critically ill.

*Sitting: (from the left) Valli, Sigmund and Tommy Huppert.*
*Standing: Hilde Huppert, Jenny Citron and Hella. Ivonitz, May 1940*

IN IVONITCH WE LIVED in two rooms, which we rented from a
Polish peasant, Maria Kenerova, a devout Catholic who treated us
with the utmost courtesy. Later on, when we had grown to know
one another well, she said to me, "Mrs. Huppert, whenever I'm in
church I pray to the Lord Jesus to watch over you all."

We managed to keep contacts with Walter, who was in Haifa,
through our cousin who lived in Hungary, which was at that period
neutral, and our relatives who lived in Cleveland, Ohio. Through
this tricky mail my husband informed me, in the spring of 1940,
that he had sent Tommy and me ship tickets to a certain Italian
shipping company in Cracow. I asked my sister, Rega, to inquire if
the tickets reached the office. She had found out that the company
was holding our tickets to Palestine. Hastily hiring a farmer and
his cart, Tommy and I made our way to Krosno. From there (again
without our armbands) we took the train to Cracow.

It took me a good deal of knocking before my sister opened the door.

"Hilde! Tommy! How good to see you, and how sad. Come in, come in!" I could hardly recognize Rega: skinny and pale. My charming sister had turned into an aging woman, attuned to hardship, slowly losing the will for survival.

"I didn't open at once," she whispered, "because it might have been a search. They come around all the time, and if you don't answer the door, they sometimes give up and try the neighbors. They take everything: the furniture, the carpets, the pictures, sewing machines, pianos, and clothing. And if anyone resists, he's beaten up or shot."

Her daughter, Ruthy, was seated silently in a corner. Tommy went over to her and they began to chat together in undertones.

The following morning I went to the shipping company and applied for the tickets Walter had sent us. They were in fact there, but the Italian visas hadn't yet arrived. I managed to find a talented lawyer, who arranged a German exit permit for a fee of 500 zlotys. My luggage was checked and cleared at customs, but that same evening the customs official arrived at Rega's apartment together with a German officer and demanded to check our baggage once again. They opened the sealed suitcases and removed a few valuables and items of clothing.

"Bon voyage, madam!" the official said politely. "It would be best not to mention our discreet visit."

Weeks went by with no sign of the Italian visas. By June 1940, when Italy joined the war on the side of the Axis Powers and the Nazis closed down the offices of the Adriatica Shipping Company (claiming it was transporting illegal passengers), I realized that we wouldn't be sailing to Palestine.

Once I made up my mind to return to Ivonitch, Rega begged me to take Ruthy with me.

"She's blonde and could pass as a Pole."

"Of course she could!" I said, looking at my sister's radiant dark "Jewish" eyes, which Ruthy had inherited. And so three of us returned to Ivonitch. From now on I had two children to care for.

BACK IN IVONITCH, I found Sigmund extremely depressed. He was deeply shocked by the sudden defeat of the French army and was agonizing over the fall of Paris. A Polish newspaper from Krosno was quoting the boastful claims of German generals who predicted that they would be marching through the streets of London within six weeks.

My sisters were dispersed: Rosa in Chrzanow, Rachel in Czestochowa (renowned for its ancient monastery and the Black Madonna). Rachel wrote to me that she and her family had been moved into a suburb now restricted solely to Jews. It was known by the newly resurrected medieval term "ghetto." No one could leave its boundaries without permission. She ended her letter with a desperate request: "Can you send us any food?"

We packed some flour, brown sugar, a jar of goose fat, sweets for the children, and a few other necessities. Our Polish landlady sent the package off from the local post office. From then on it became a weekly routine: parcels to Czestochowa as well to various other places.

Rosa's husband had been arrested in Chrzanow during the first few weeks of German occupation and had been sent, together with other Jewish men, to forced labor in an industrial complex near a place called Auschwitz. My sister Rosa, who was both beautiful and courageous, ignored the advice of her friends and set out in pursuit of her husband. She was lucky. A certain German overseer, impressed by her beauty (and by the sum of money she slipped him), was willing to erase a name from the work list. Rosa and her husband were soon on their way back to Chrzanow. On arriving home they recited *Birkas Hagomel*, the traditional blessing for deliverance from mortal danger.

Much of the Chrzanow region was by now annexed to the Greater Reich. In the early 1940s the Jews in this region enjoyed certain privileges, such as ration cards that enabled them to buy goods at official prices. However, this didn't last for long. The Nazis began detaining the wealthy Jews, and after some time, their families would be officially informed that nearest and dearest had somehow succumbed to typhus and that the ashes of the deceased could be obtained for a symbolic fee of ten deutschmark.

Our relatives, mostly confined to the ghettos, strove to find some kind of employment in hope that hard work might save their lives and those of their dependents. At that time nobody could imagine that there was a systematic plan of genocide carefully being carried out. Conditions would get much worse for the Jews of Poland when Germany launched its surprise offensive on its Russian ally in June 1941.

# Chapter 2
## TEMPORARY HAVEN

*T*HERE WERE ONLY about twenty Jews, mainly women and children, in the village of Ivonitch, where we had found refuge; most of the Jewish men had fled toward the Russian border. The new regime was quick to move in. A German Kommandant arrived in our midst with strict orders to impose the anti-Jewish regulations. His first edict was the expulsion of all the Jews from Ivonitch to the Krosno ghetto.

My father-in-law quickly consulted with Olesh, the local Polish chief of police, with whom he had struck up a friendship by translating documents from the German. This time the meeting was formal and reserved. The police chief claimed that most of his authority had been taken away and that decisions were now in the hands of the German Kommandant.

"However, it's rumored that one can 'grease his palm.'"

Knowing this, I paid a call to the Kommandant bearing gifts (a few items of clothing we had taken with us from Teschen). After ogling the silk shirt, the knitted socks, and the cravat, he stowed them away in a drawer of his desk before offering me a seat. Then he asked me just what it was I wanted.

Using my best German I told him something of our family

history and asked for a permit to remain in Ivonitch. His response was totally unexpected: "I have no objection to all the Jews of Ivonitch staying here in the meantime. Gestapo headquarters in Krosno is occupied with far more important matters. If this is all you request, I can delay issuing the order."

He rose; so did I, with a sudden feeling of immense relief, happiness almost, before responsibility crowded in again: I knew I had to make the most of this moment.

"May I be permitted, sir, to bring in a few members of my family who are in Cracow?"

"How many?" I had to make a quick decision, not to overdo it, but at the same time to save as many as I could.

"My mother Bluma Biegeleisen, my sister and her husband, Rega and Marcus Hauben, and…".

"Just how many?" His voice, like a whiplash, froze my tongue. I waited for him to speak again.

"You may bring those three you have mentioned. My secretary will prepare the appropriate documents. You see, we are not the monsters you think we are!"

And then he gave a brief, harsh, frightening laugh. It was a laugh I could still hear echoing as I made my way down the main road and up the hill to where we lived. I walked as fast as I could, the good news and the ugly laughter mingling in my ears:

*"I have no objection to all the Jews staying here in the meantime."* What about later?

It was a joyful reunion: Mama, Rega, and Marcus. Mama, who had always been a hard worker, soon began to play active part in running the household and taking care of both Tommy and Ruthy. The two children would play together and often roam in the woods that bordered our backyard.

I FIRST HEARD the term "transport" in Krosno, mumbled in undertones by officials of the Judenrat. Nobody knew any details of where the people were being sent or what happened to them later on. Letters from Warsaw told us that each of the deportees was given three loaves of bread and a jar of honey and that the official version claimed that they were being relocated to factory work in Eastern Europe. Rachel wrote from Czestochowa that the Judenrat had been ordered to conduct a census of the entire ghetto and that everyone should prepare for a transport.

"All the ghetto is in panic," she wrote. "I can confide in you, dearest Hilde, I'm also terrified. Greetings to you all and kisses for Mama, for Rega, and for the kids. My only comfort is that you're all safe and together."

Not long after I was summoned before the German Kommandant. I went armed with gifts from Sigmund's emergency reserve, but the Kommandant ignored the parcel I placed on his desk.

"I want to show you something," he said.

It was a document bearing the stamp of the Gestapo from Krosno, an order to all the Jews in all the villages in the region to decamp to the ghetto in Rymanov.

"Maybe…maybe…" I stammered.

"This time I am helpless." He extended his hand. "Tomorrow morning I must publish this edict and see that it is carried out…with no exceptions. Sorry."

At home I took Sigmund aside and told him of the Kommandant's warning. He was silent for a moment, passing a hand across his brow and stroking his clipped moustache, before giving precise instructions:

"You must go back to the Kommandant. Ask him to phone Gestapo headquarters in Krosno and inquire whether Czechs are also being deported. Implore him not to mention the word Jews."

"I'm not sure he'll agree to play your game."

"He said he was sorry. So let's give it a try!"

The Kommandant was somewhat surprised to see me again, nevertheless he heard my plea.

"Jewish guile!" he remarked when he caught on to what Sigmund was hinting at. "Tricky business. Very risky."

"I'm sure your honor has faced greater risks." (I ventured a little flattery.)

"*Aber natuerlich!*" he snorted. "Deporting Czechs, right? Just Czechs."

As he posed Sigmund's carefully phrased question over the phone to Gestapo headquarters, I could clearly hear a furious voice on the other end:

"Imbecile! Whoever told you to deport Czechs?" and he immediately hung up.

"Imbecile, indeed!"

The Kommandant grunted and promptly issued permits for all of the family who held Czech citizenship to remain in Ivonitch. Rega and her husband, however, along with the other Jews of the region, were forced to depart for Rymanov. Mrs. Kenerova, our landlady, hid Mama and Ruthy in her attic.

AUGUST 1942, a warm summer's day on which a hasty note arrived from Marcus: "Disaster! Hilde. Get to Rymanov as quick as you can. I've been conscripted to a work brigade."

This time, too, Sigmund suggested appealing to Mr. Olesh, who had often gone out of his way to help the Jews. The police chief proposed to escort me personally to Rymanov.

"If they see you with me, in uniform, they won't ask for your papers."

My thanks were dismissed with a shrug of the shoulders, as if to say "What else can I do?"

We set out on foot along winding hill roads almost devoid of people. On reaching Rymanov we first called on a Polish police officer with whom Mr. Olesh was acquainted. When I asked about the "work brigade" and Marcus, he told us the whole story of the liquidation of the ghetto.

"The chief of the Krosno Gestapo was here a few days ago and wanted the Judenrat to hand out a huge sum of money along with fifty pairs of boots and quite a few bolts of cloth. This 'ransom,' he promised, would prevent deportation. The Judenrat did all that it could, and the money and the goods were delivered to the Gestapo on time. People felt better when the Judenrat chairman returned from Krosno; they all flocked to the cemetery to honor the graves of the righteous, utter thanks for this 'miracle,' and pray for mercy and deliverance.

"Five thirty the next morning the entire ghetto was surrounded by S.S. troops and the Gestapo. The Jews were given half an hour to assemble in the marketplace, and they were informed that anyone found hiding in his home would be shot on the spot. They were all there on time.

"They were ordered to line up in threes and kneel down. They knelt. The S.S. men walked through the ranks kicking people here and there."

Our host paused for a moment, but Olesh urged him to continue.

"They were ordered to hand over their money and jewelry. Afterwards, the guards separated the children, the elderly, and the invalids from the rest of them. The troops shoved them onto trucks and they were driven off. About an hour later the trucks were back – empty, bloodstained.

"They told the chairman of the Judenrat that a hundred young men, who were working as road builders, wouldn't be deported; I suspect your brother-in-law must have been in that group. Then the Gestapo chief wanted to keep back some fifty young women who worked in the neighborhood. But one of the Polish village heads claimed he didn't want any Jewish women under his jurisdiction, so that was that as far as the women were concerned.

"In the middle of all this, one of the Jews suddenly gets to his feet: Dr. Fink, about forty years old. He stands there pointing a finger at the Gestapo, yelling at them: 'Assassins! Criminals! Predators! You will pay for these crimes. You may have subdued us helpless Jews, but you are going to lose this war against England and America and Russia! I am proud to have been born a Jew. I am proud to die as an honest man! I don't envy you Germans…Your fate is sealed!'

"The Germans seemed startled for a moment, maybe even confused by such an outburst; then their commander gave them a signal and three soldiers were on the doctor with their rifle butts, beating the poor man to death. I can still see him collapsing.

"The chief of Gestapo offered the Judenrat chairman sanctuary in the Krosno Ghetto, for himself and his family, but Mr. Shapiro refused and was shipped off with the rest of his people.

"Late in the afternoon, the hundreds of men and women, still in the square, were ordered to form rows of five. German troops marched them off to the railway station where a train of cattle cars was waiting in a siding. The soldiers herded them on board and barred the doors. I've no idea how many perished inside: It was a hot day and they had no water. That train was parked there for two days and nights. When I asked why they weren't moving them out, I was told they were waiting for another transport from Krosno.

"Those fellows in the 'work brigade' you were asking about are being housed in an old schoolhouse just outside of the town. I can help you get there. I'd like to help, I really would." His wife came in at this point, serving steaming cups of coffee.

"Bring a bottle of vodka and three glasses. The lady will also take a drink, she looks as if she needs it."

Once the dutiful wife had served the drinks and again vanished into the kitchen, our Polish host blurted out, "The S.S. were slaughtering infants, smashing babies' heads against telegraph poles. Don't be angry, madam, that I'm telling you all this. I'm a devout Catholic. I just can't understand how they could do that."

Mr. Olesh was holding my arm, supporting me as we walked

our way out of the town. After about an hour we arrived at a long, low, thatched building with broken windows and gaps in the roof. Recognizing the Polish officer, two guards unlocked the door and admitted us into a seemingly endless corridor. At first I couldn't see a thing; I only heard muffled mumblings and groaning. A sickening stench of sweat and urine filled the air. Mr. Olesh, seeing I was about to faint, suggested we step outside. Declining his offer, I went into the first of the rooms. There were about twenty men in there, some strewn on straw pallets, others just squatting on the floor, heads in hand, gazing into the non-existent distance. One of them was mumbling in a monotone, as if praying:

"So hot…it was so hot…they sealed the cattle cars and they were all inside. Feigele, little Nachum, Itzik…you could see the steam coming out of the air vents. We were on the outside…they were on the inside…Feigele, little Nachum, Itzik…so hot…it was so hot…"

I made my way between those tortured faces whose dulled eyes betrayed the insupportable agony within. Dwelling endlessly on the fate of their women and children was bringing them to the brink of madness.

In the second room one of the men recognized me; struggling to his feet he whispered: "Marcus is there, in the corner by the window. He's not at all well, Madam Hilde, he's ill, very ill."

I could barely recognize my brother-in-law. He lay sprawled on a stinking mattress, delirious and raging with fever. Only after I had repeated his name several times did he finally turn his head and gaze vaguely in my direction.

"Hilde…you are here. Rega's gone. She's gone. I wanted to go with her, to die with her…they wouldn't let me. They said the women would be safe…promised us we'd see each other again. They were lying. I'll never see Rega again."

"Ruthy is safe with me," I tried to calm him. "She's fine. Ruthy and Tommy are both fine."

"That's good, Hilde. Ruthy and Tommy at least. And you. Before they took Rega she said to me, 'There's no justice or righteousness anymore. No miracles.' She gave me this ring, she'd managed to keep hidden…for Ruthy. 'I'll not be needing rings,' she said, 'I've not got the will to live anymore.' Take the ring Hilde, give it to Ruthy. Say goodbye to her…from me and from Rega."

Once more Marcus was drifting off into delirium. As I put some of the food I had brought with me under his mattress he suddenly became lucid again: "When they took Rega away, they took my heart too…on this train. Some of the fellows wanted to send someone to follow the transport, to find out where it was going. What's the use? No one comes back from there. Hilde, what are we punished for? Why does God let this happen?"

I could offer Marcus little comfort; my anguish was as great as his. I had grown up with Rega, sharing our joys and our sorrows. I loved my sister. I sat beside him for some time trying to sooth his seething brow, but I had nothing to say. Then Olesh came in, indicating that we had to leave. Marcus was delirious again, so I fled.

ON OUR WAY BACK HOME we walked swiftly and in silence. It was only when we neared our destination that I begged Mr. Olesh not to say anything to my father-in-law. I told him that I needed a few days before I could face the family with what I had experienced in Rymanov.

But when we got back to Ivonitch, Mama already knew. While I was away a postcard had arrived for me from Rega:

"Dearest Hilde, I'm at the railway station. One of the workers here has taken pity on us and agreed to post this for me. A last request: look after Ruthy and Mama…Forget me and enjoy life. There's no point in saying au revoir. Death is too close. All my love. Rega."

Mama was silent all the rest of the day. Only in the evening, after she had tucked the children into bed, did she ask me to tell her what I had seen in Rymanov. All of a sudden, it burst forth: the entire story in all its appalling detail. Mama wept silently for a long while before she finally spoke: "I was hidden, Rega taken."

The following day our landlady brought me a letter from my second sister, Rosa. She wrote that she and her family were about to be deported from Chrzanow to an unknown destination: "As we're employed in the workshops we could have been spared, but we chose to join the deportation so as not to be separated from Romek." Romek was their only child.

A few days later, another letter. This time from my eldest sister, Rachel, in Czenstochow:

"Last sign of life; it's good to know that at least you, my dearest, might survive to see the day of vengeance come. If this ever really happens…remember us. Hilde, kiss Mama for me, and all our family. Your sister, Rachel."

Mama appeared to accept these bitter tidings quite stoically. It was only late at night, when she thought everyone was asleep, that I could hear her passionate prayers and her stifled sobs. During the day she was busy taking care of her grandchild, Ruthy. The two were hidden in the attic, only daring to venture down into the apartment after dark behind tightly-locked doors and securely-closed shutters.

We got many such farewell letters from relatives and friends. There were few who managed to acquire forged documents, which enabled them to pass themselves as Aryans. Other more defiant souls joined the ranks of the partisans in the forests.

There was no sign of the aid we had all hoped for from the Allied Powers.

AUTUMN 1942: Axe-blows from the outside where the landlady's son is splitting logs for the winter fires. Jenny and I are knitting stockings for the children. Sigmund is reading a favorite book. Suddenly we could hear a car grinding its way up the hill. Hastily sounding a warning to Mama and Ruthy, I resume my knitting as calmly as possible. I hear footsteps and men's voices, from outside. Then, following, ingratiating tones of our friend, Mr. Scheller (chairman of the village council) and an unfamiliar, guttural intonation. The sounds draw nearer; the door is flung open, and on the threshold stands an officer of the Gestapo, two Polish policemen, and Mr. Scheller. My father-in-law lays aside his book with a polite greeting. Mr. Scheller, about to reply, is silenced by an icy glance from the Gestapo.

"What's this I see here?" he sneered. "A Jewish family sitting comfortably at home. The woman is knitting, and the man reading a book while we in Krosno are led to believe that this region has been thoroughly cleansed?"

"We are Czech citizens," I tried to explain.

"Hold your tongue, woman! Speak when you are spoken to! Now listen to my orders and obey them. Fast. I haven't got all day. Within five minutes I want to see all your jewelry here on the table. Maybe you've got a collection of valuable stamps you're hiding away somewhere? The Reich needs all of them!"

As we laid out our jewelry along with Sigmund's precious stamp album, the Polish police rifled through our rooms. Bed linen, underwear, and clothing were dragged out and flung into the truck that waited outside. Then came the turn of the Persian rug, the crystal, and the china.

This Gestapo officer (whose name I later learned was Romanski and came from Jaslo), then ordered the confiscation of two suitcases packed with food that had been sent to us by relatives in the United States. When I pointed out that these arrived through official channels and had been cleared by the German authorities in Krosno, he promised to look into the matter.

"In any case," he yelled at us, "you won't be here much longer!"

Within a moment the officer was gone, followed by the Polish police and the hapless Mr. Scheller.

A week later, Mr. Scheller and the same two Polish policemen were back, bringing with them the two suitcases. Mr. Scheller explained that the Gestapo officer, upon finding that my claim was officially correct, had ordered the goods returned. The Nazis were extremely wary of anything involving foreign powers or agencies. Had the Allied Powers been aware of this and flexed a bit of muscle in this arena of influence, perhaps many Jews might have been saved.

The pillaged rooms and Gestapo threats took their toll. We lived in dread, fearing that deportation was not far away. Few Jews remained in the entire region. Some were crammed in the Krosno Ghetto, others in the Rymanov labor camp, which, rumor had it, was destined for liquidation.

It had been three months since my sisters and their families had been deported, and we had had no word from them. I begged Police Chief Olesh to try and find out the fate of those who had been shoved onto the trains at Rymanov. When he contacted a few astonished colleagues in Krosno, he was advised to mind his own business. All they knew was that the transports had been routed via Rawa-Ruska in the direction of Belzec and that at that point, the trail went dead. There were whispered rumors in Krosno about camps with gas chambers into which the Jews were crowded and gassed.

Police Chief Olesh dismissed this as nothing more than malicious gossip. We wanted to believe him, clinging to the hope that our relatives were, in fact, alive and working in a labor camp of distant Eastern Europe and simply unable to write to us.

Fearing the ever approaching threat of deportation, I decided to place Ruthy in the orphanage of a Catholic convent for safekeep-

*Ruthy and Tommy. Ivonitz, March 1941*

ing some twelve kilometers (seven miles) outside Ivonitch. Mr. Scheller's wife volunteered to accompany me. "The Mother Superior knows our family and won't let me down," she said.

The Mother Superior greeted us in a spacious room, its walls adorned with a silver crucifix and an ancient oil painting depicting the Virgin Mary holding the Holy Infant. Once Mrs. Scheller had introduced me as a Polish friend who had come with a request, the Abbess indicated that I could now speak.

"There's a Jewish girl hiding in my house. Her parents have been deported. Would you agree to accept her into your orphanage?"

The Mother Superior made no reply.

"She's six years old, she's fair haired. Her mother left me enough money to cover your expenses."

There was an exchange of glances between the Abbess and Mrs. Scheller.

"The child's life is in danger." I was almost imploring her by now. "If you must, you can baptize her. But please, after this war is over, inform her relatives in the United States. I have the address."

Brushing aside my outstretched hand she replied in a calm but firm voice, "We have no interest in saving Jewish heretics."

"Reverend Mother," I appealed to her, "even our Jesus Christ was born a Jew, and it is written in the Holy Bible 'Love thy neighbor as thyself.'" The Mother Superior turned her icy gaze upon me for just a moment before gesturing to Mrs. Scheller that the interview was over.

Ruthy Hauben died along with my mother, Bluma Biegeleisen, in the summer of 1943. She was, by then, eight years old.

The convent is situated in the village of Miesce Piastowa, which lies between Krosno and Ivonitch.

LIVING WITH US AT THE TIME was Tommy's Czech nanny, Hella, whom Sigmund had brought with us from Teschen. When an edict was issued forbidding Jews to employ Christians, she went to work for the local pharmacy, which had been taken over by a Pole after its Jewish owner fled. This new pharmacist soon amassed a small fortune as the cost of medicine skyrocketed during the war.

Hella was now taking care of this man's son and working as cleaning woman in the pharmacy. She still lived at our place and we remained good friends. One evening she told us of an incident she had overheard while sweeping up. A little five-year-old girl had come in to use the scale. The pharmacist recognized her since she had been there before with her mother.

"And what's your name, little girl?" he asked as he set her on the scale.

"Eva Maria."

"And before that?" he said in a fatherly tone.

"Malvinka," she muttered. And then, with downcast eyes as if caught red-handed, she bolted from the pharmacy. The Pole exchanged a glance with his wife as if his suspicions had been proven.

"What are you hanging around for?" the pharmacist suddenly yelled at Hella. "We don't pay you for eavesdropping on your employers!"

It was Sigmund's opinion that the child's mother should be warned, and Aunt Jenny took upon herself this somewhat embarrassing mission.

On hearing what Hella had overheard, the girl's mother turned pale. The little girl was lying on her bed, holding back her tears, convinced she was in for a scolding. Instead, her mother drew her into a warm embrace: "You're always my Malvinka. It wasn't your fault...Mama isn't upset with you."

Turning to my aunt she added, "We are Jews from Lvov. The Germans shot my husband and my family was deported. Only me and Malvinka were left. I managed to get hold of Aryan papers and we've been passing ourselves as Poles. This is our fourth hiding place so far, but whenever it seems to be safe, something else happens and we've got to get away again. Believe me, madam, if it wasn't for Malvinka I'd have put an end to myself long ago. I've got no strength left anymore, and the money and the valuables are running out...It's all for Malvinka."

NOVEMBER 14, 1942: Tomorrow would be a joint birthday for both Sigmund and myself. We had celebrated this together for seven years now. Mama got up in the middle of the night to secretly bake her usual cake. We were planning a birthday party for the following evening; it would be a little fun for Tommy and Ruthy.

That afternoon Police Chief Olesh had a visit from a Gestapo officer, who demanded to be taken to our place.

"I've come to take those Jews to Krosno."

Fearing that the Gestapo might discover Mama and Ruthy, Mr.

Olesh played for time, offering his visitor a glass of schnapps. He reassured him that he could save him the trouble.

"I can bring you all four to Krosno tomorrow morning."

"Fair enough. Ten o'clock prompt. That climb up the hill to their place is ruining my car. When will you people ever learn to build decent roads?"

"At your orders, sir."

"Just another mission. I've had a word there's a Jewish woman hiding in this village with a daughter posing as honest Poles."

"Sir?"

"You didn't know that? You're chief of the police, Olesh! You're responsible for this village, damn fool! Go to the pharmacy, buy yourself an aspirin, and have a chat with the pharmacist. He'll give you a clue. You've got three days to hand them over. I'll accept no excuses! One more thimbleful of schnapps and I'll be on my way. It's tiring to do business with you Poles."

Good Mr. Olesh came to us immediately, bearing the bad tidings.

"There's just one hope, that once they've checked your papers they might let you go."

Little comfort in that; we all knew full well that a Gestapo summons for all four of us meant more than a routine examination of our documents.

In the evening Mama descended from her attic refuge bearing the birthday cake.

"I know. I heard what Mr. Olesh had to say. Now come children, light the candles, then we'll all pray together. And you, Sigmund, tonight I'll use your Hebrew name, Shlomo, if you've no objection."

"No objection, Bluma. But you'll have to teach me the Hebrew prayer."

# Chapter 3
## PRISON

THE FOLLOWING DAY Sigmund, Aunt Jenny, Tommy, and I (my mother-in-law, Valli, had died two years earlier), were driven by Olesh to Krosno. We all carried Czech passports. It was cold and raining when we got there, and as we arrived ahead of time, Mr. Olesh took us to a certain Mr. Schachner, a Jewish garage owner. Schachner did maintenance jobs for the German vehicles and was therefore permitted to live outside the confines of the ghetto. He also acted as part-time chauffeur for the German Kommandant, with whom he was on quite good terms. We told Mr. Schachner about our summons to Gestapo headquarters and asked whether he might be able to put in a good word for us. Tommy, then aged six, voiced his own plea:

"Please do your best, Mr. Schachner. Don't forget about us!"

"I've got a son just your age, so I'll remember you all right."

Mr. Schachner suggested that we leave with him any valuables we had on us.

"I'll take good care of your things…the Gestapo, they'll grab everything."

At the Gestapo headquarters the officer in charge received us with unconcealed satisfaction.

"You've had it easy so far, but you can forget about all that now on! Hand over your papers and fill out these forms."

We did so. Noting the dates, the officer commented dryly that my father-in-law and I had chosen a fine way to celebrate our birthdays. After being registered, we were all searched; they were looking for valuables and cash. Then Aunt Jenny and I were assigned to the women's cells, Sigmund and Tommy to the men's, except that Tommy was clinging to my skirt, refusing to be separated. For some reason, the prison guard took pity on us and let him stay with me. So Sigmund was marched off alone.

THE KEYS RASPED as the iron door was locked behind us; it was a small, dank cell. Jenny and I were feeling very disheartened; only Tommy seemed to be in good spirits, certain that Mr. Schachner would keep to his word and somehow get us out of there. (Several weeks later we heard that Schachner had obtained Hungarian papers and had left Poland with his family, and most likely, with the remains of our valuables.)

The door wasn't opened again until some time in the evening, when a warden handed us a bowl of cabbage soup. He was back within the hour, laughing at us when he saw we hadn't touched the foul-smelling brew. "In a day or two you'll be begging for it!" he muttered.

We made some kind of bed for Tommy out of my overcoat, and then Jenny and I sat ourselves on the narrow wooden bench. The straw mattresses were crawling with lice.

It was a very silent first night in prison.

The following morning they added an elderly woman to our cell. We made room for her on the bench, and she huddled herself up into the corner without a word, seemingly sunken in her sorrows.

Jenny drew my attention to an eye peering at us through the spy hole in the door. Then we heard a woman in the corridor speaking in Polish:

"Give me that sweater of yours."

"Why should I?" I replied. "It's cold in here and it's the only one I've got."

"You'd best be giving it to me. You won't be needing it much longer."

I didn't answer, but the eye remained glued to the spy hole. After a few minutes of this we heard loud voices in the distance and the hurried shuffle of feet moving away from the door. The woman, whoever she was, had gone.

Once it was quiet again, our cellmate said, "I'd like to talk. Would you care to listen?" Her wrinkled face had a softer look as she turned to us and began her tale:

"I was born into a traditional Jewish home in Chrzanow. My mother died giving birth to me, so I was raised by my grandmother. She was an embittered old woman who blamed me for the death of her beloved daughter. She used to yell at me all the time and curse her own misfortune. When I was twelve I was put to work in my father's tavern here in Krosno scrubbing the floors and scouring the filthy wooden tables. I can still remember the sickening stench of the place."

I began to wonder why she was telling us all this, but it seemed impossible to interrupt her once she started. It was a story that was to go on for days on end.

"At the tavern I got to know a platform attendant from the railway station. He used to wear a sharp uniform and had decent table manners. He'd always smile at me, slip me a tip when I brought him his mug of beer, and lay a hand on me whenever he could. I didn't mind, but one day my father saw him doing it, and he dragged me behind the bar and slapped my face good and hard. After that I got even more attached to that fellow from the station. He used to tell me how beautiful I was, that he was in love with me and wanted to marry me.

"In the end, I ran off with him to Lvov, where he introduced me into a convent so I could be baptized and prepare for marriage. My father tried everything he could to get me back. He used to sit for hours outside the convent gates begging the sisters to let him see me, but they wouldn't. No, that's not true, it was I who refused to see him.

"After I was baptized, we were married in a Catholic church and came back to Krosno. People told me that my father sat in mourning for me seven days, as is the Jewish custom, and had fallen ill with a broken heart. Poor father. He died only a few months after I was married, and I was suddenly overcome with remorse. I blamed my husband of course. I used to taunt him and would always burst into tears. I even took to drinking on the sly. Naturally, he started staying out late at night. Then a couple of my girlfriends told me he was playing around with the new barmaid.

"That's when I began to sober up, began to realize I was ruining my life. So we patched things up and had two kids, a boy and a girl. Neither of them knew anything of my past. My daughter looked like her dad, my son was dark haired and looked like me. I noticed that the girl only made friends with Christian girls, while the boy sometimes used to bring Jewish kids home as well. My son married a Jewish girl, they're living in Warsaw. My daughter, who works for the municipality, married a teacher, a Pole.

"I can tell fortunes, you know, with the cards, and read your palm. I learned how from a woman who was always drunk in my father's tavern. One day I read the cards for a neighbor of ours, and when everything I told her came true, she was telling everyone about it. So then lots of people were coming to me, asking advice, wanting their futures told. I'd tell them what I saw, and they'd pay quite well.

"My husband died a few years before the war broke out. My son-in-law, the teacher, was called up to the Polish army when the war started and later on, became a prisoner of war. I used to get a pension from the railway until the German invasion. As they canceled the monthly payments the three of us (my daughter, her daughter, and myself), we were living on my daughter's salary and what I made by fortune telling. It was my daughter who suggested that I try and get the railway pension renewed by applying to the German authorities. When we got the forms, there was one clause that demanded proof of the "Aryan origin of the entire family." That's when I had to tell my daughter about my Jewish background. She got very upset, said she feared for my life, and that now she could understand why I used to smuggle food parcels into the ghetto. My daughter changed. She began to identify with the sufferings of the Jews and did her best to help. She risked her life more than once.

"A few days ago, when my daughter was at work, this Gestapo fellow comes to the apartment and starts yelling at me, 'Come on, you old Jewish hag! I'm taking you to where you belong…among your brethren.'

"I've no idea how the Germans found out. Maybe they began to be suspicious when we didn't return the forms on time; maybe somebody drew conclusions, asked questions."

The old woman was also able to tell us a lot about what was actually going on in Krosno. Her daughter heard from her boss in the municipality about the forthcoming plans for transports and the liquidation of the ghetto.

IT WAS FROM my fellow prisoner's ramblings that I managed to piece together the fate of a friend of mine, Mrs. Hausner, whose husband had managed to flee to Russia at the outbreak of the war. Mrs. Hausner had remained behind to manage the family café called the Bristol. One day the Gestapo ordered the Judenrat to provide two women to prepare a party at the local Kommandant's residence. The Judenrat sent Mrs. Hausner and another waitress from the Café Bristol. The two women worked quietly and efficiently until the Polish cook, who had worked for Mrs. Hausner before the war, suddenly recognized her former employer and began using foul language, which was deliberately ignored. Such apparent indifference seems to have been too much for the cook. Ripping off her apron, she ran into the reception room where, upon finding the Kommandant, she blurted out that the lying Jewess working in his home had always slandered the Fuehrer and claimed that Germany was going to lose the war.

Mrs. Hausner, who had just completed her chores, was astonished by a blow from a trooper, who hauled her off to face the Kommandant, and by the mocking laughter of the Polish cook. The second waitress was sent back to the ghetto and immediately reported the incident to the Judenrat. Despite the fact that these were day-to-day occurrences, the chairman nevertheless found some courage and went to the Gestapo headquarters, where the officer in charge reassured him that Mrs. Hausner would be released within a few days.

In the meantime, the Kommandant's banquet was turning out to be a roaring success. The officers and their various companions were digging voraciously into the delicacies and were showering their praises on the tasteful arrangements. They were all eating ravenously and drinking heartily. Some of the S.S. and the Gestapo became playful and suggested live target practice. Four female Jewish prisoners were dragged from their cells and ordered to strip naked, while the intoxicated Nazis drew their guns. The women fell one by one; some of the guests applauded, others turned aside. The next day the Judenrat was ordered to clear some corpses from the scene of the party: one of them was that of Mrs. Hausner.

JENNY AND I would sit and listen to the tales of the old lady, whereas Tommy tried to avoid her, afraid of her piercing glance.

"She's like a witch, Mama," he said, just before falling asleep.

One day I, too, could sense her piercing eyes. I tried to say something, but was silenced by a bony finger she held up to her lips. The woman then began to speak in a dull monotone that seemed to emerge out of the depths:

"You will never go home. You will witness many happenings. Keep this child always at your side. Far away across the seas your husband awaits you. I see a tall man. It will be a long time before you meet. But you will. I can see you running into his outstretched arms. There's an old woman in the house, weeping, but she will be of help. This evening you get a visit, a visitor for you. Someone in uniform, but not a soldier."

I could hardly hear these last words, but then of a sudden she straightened up as if awakening from a deep sleep.

"What…what was I saying?" she asked. When I told her, word for word, she assured me that it would all come true.

Anxious and expectant, we waited for the day to end. At six in the evening the cabbage soup was served; once that had been dealt with, it was lights out, and the reign of night began. The town clock chimed seven, then eight, but no one came.

"Maybe tomorrow," I consoled the old woman as I bid her goodnight.

"He'll come. He'll be here!" she insisted, as if in a frenzy.

At about nine o'clock there were footsteps in the corridor, a key in the lock, a light of a torch, and the warden's voice: "Hilde Huppert, out at once! Visitor."

Rushing out of the cell I found that this welcome visitor was Police Chief Olesh. He brought us a bottle of milk, a loaf of bread, and a pat of butter.

"Your mother," he whispered, "gave me some money to try and help you at the Gestapo headquarters. I told the clerk who is handling your files that you've got entry visas to Palestine on the way, and he said that in that case you'd be all right."

"On the way," I replied bitterly, "but not yet here."

I went on to thank Mr. Olesh from the bottom of my heart, begging him to tell me about Mama and Ruthy.

"So far, so good. Mrs. Kenerova is keeping them hidden, but I don't know how long she'll be able to hold out. It's a very risky business."

Back in the cell, bearing greetings from Mama and the food she had sent, we were almost joyful. Tommy got a slice of bread and butter and a swig of milk. When I offered the old woman a slice of bread she giggled before biting into it. "Just like crossing my palm with silver, isn't it?"

It was hard for me to fall asleep that night. I was seized by a sudden, irrational hope.

*"A visitor...someone in uniform...but not a soldier."*

I kept repeating the part of her prophecy that had come true. What would be with the rest of it?

THE NEXT MORNING Aunt Jenny presented her palm for a reading. After a brief glance, the old woman swept her hand aside, mumbling something about "having lost the touch."

Another day, seated on the wooden bench as usual, Aunt Jenny noticed some kind of tapping on the wall. We both listened closely, but couldn't decipher the code. This is how we discovered the "Jungle Telegraph" of the prison. By pressing an ear to the drainpipe one could hear echoing conversations transmitted from cell to cell, updated information about everything that was going on with regards old and new prisoners alike.

"The Jewish woman and that kid are still with us." This was the deeper of the two voices. "I reckoned they'd have been polished off long ago."

"Don't lose any sleep over it." This was the hoarse one. "They soon will be."

Once, during this eerie sort of eavesdropping, we heard the deeper voice saying, "I've got a nasty feeling they're going to come for me tonight." Then he was suddenly yelling. "I'm only thirty years old. I've got a wife and two kids. I don't want to die! I haven't done anything wrong!"

We moved away from the drainpipe in a vain attempt to flee from reality.

That same night we were awakened by distant shouting: we could recognize the deep voice from the drainpipe. He seemed to be struggling with his jailers. Then there was the sound of blows and the dragging of an inert body down the corridor. When first light filtered palely through the tiny window, set high in the wall of our cell, we heard a few shots.

THURSDAY, DECEMBER 4, 1942, after barely three weeks of incarceration, which already seemed like a lifetime: I was again summoned from my cell. Police Chief Olesh was awaiting me in the prison office, this time with his wife. They had again brought us a food parcel. When I asked Mr. Olesh about our chances of being released, he was evasive, mumbling something about our situation not being very "bright," but voicing the belief that nothing really 'terrible" would happen to us. Mrs. Olesh was in tears as she hugged me: "Your Mama and little Ruthy are still all right. Try not to worry, dear Hilde."

At six o'clock the next morning the door of our cell was kicked open by a screaming S.S. officer.

"Three minutes! *Raus!*"

We hastily got into our clothes and were led out into the prison yard. There we met Sigmund. The once dapper tradesman now looked like a wizened old man. He bent down to kiss Tommy and then straightened up to clasp hands with both Jenny and myself. We were marched to the ghetto, with the winter wind and snowflakes lashing at our faces.

When the gates of the ghetto were opened, we saw people lined up in ranks, surrounded by Gestapo militiamen. We were ordered to stand in line with one of the groups and wait. It was clear now: we had been listed for transport.

I could see what appeared to be a family of four approaching a Gestapo officer. He listened imperiously for a few minutes before drawing his pistol and shooting the husband, wife and both children. I later learned that the man had worked at the Krosno airfield and had refused to be parted from his family. By slaying them together the German officer seemed to have solved the problem.

They ordered us to form up in threes. Then the Germans began to set a fast pace towards the railway station. We were marched over the icy ground with the snowflakes still whipping at our ears. Some fell by the wayside.

At the railway station we had to wait in the freezing cold: German soldiers patrolled the platform, their menacing loose-tongued German Shepherds baring their teeth and dribbling saliva.

Much, much later, we were crowded into cattle cars – 130 apiece. We stood there together in the dark, wide-eyed, heads erect, gasping in the dense, sweaty air. Suddenly I heard Sigmund saying, "Hilde, when you first came to Teschen I feared that you had tricked our Walter. It took me some time to realize I was wrong. I've never told you this before. Can you hear me?"

"I hear you, Sigmund."

"Forgive me for those early days."

"Papa, give me your hand. Is this your hand I'm holding?"

"I'm not sure anymore, but I can feel your touch."

Only then did I realize just what this confession meant: My father-in-law was bidding me goodbye.

"Sigmund!" I was begging him. "Don't take those pills, you mustn't! You were in the army of the Kaiser. Be brave, Sigmund. We need you."

There was no answer. Then Tommy's voice broke the silence.

"Grandpa, Mama's talking to you."

"I heard her," he mumbled. "Don't worry, I'm not going away.
And in any case, I can't move."

The train was clanking its way along uneven rails. We were trying to find some way of improvising some sort of place for Tommy
to sit when a man spoke to me.

"They brought you from the prison?"

I couldn't see his face.

"True."

"So you must be starving."

Even before I could answer, this anonymous hand shoved a
knapsack across to me, which contained a quarter loaf of bread, a
bit of sausage, two apples, and a bottle of cold tea.

"But what about you?"

"Don't worry. I have friends from the ghetto who'll take care
of me."

"How can I thank you?"

"Don't bother. Eat something. The bread's quite fresh."

Now and then we stopped and could overhear chit-chat between Polish railway men and our German guards.

"How many pigs on board?"

"Couple of thousand."

"Why not finish them off with hand grenades?"

"Why waste good grenades?" (Then laughter.)

As the train was chugging its way along towards an unknown
destination another voice (speaking Yiddish) could be heard. This
was the aged Rabbi of Krosno, who also happened to be in our cattle
car. "Yidden, this is the first night of Chanukah. Despite the fact
that our Lord is testing us, we must bless that miracle."

The rabbi recited the words over a single candle, "a blessing for
the miracles and wonders of a long-forgotten age." At that moment
a woman who had been clinging to the barbed-wire hatch and
checking out the station signs as they flashed by, suddenly cried

out, "This isn't the route to Auschwitz! I know this region. They're taking us somewhere else!"

"Blessed be the Name," intoned the Rabbi. "Let us sing."

And we sang, all of us together. The good news flew from one car to the next, borne on the wings of light and song.

SHORTLY BEFORE DAWN the train slowed down and finally stopped. The doors were flung open and the Germans were again yelling at us to get out:

"*Raus! Raus!*"

Stretching our frozen, aching limbs we stumbled out into a cold, clear nightscape.

"Count off and keep silent!" The commands were in German.

After being counted we waited in silence, while some of the German guards went to drink themselves in a nearby tavern, curse their bitter fate, and in particular, curse us. Once they had got through that, the trek began. We were marched through the suburbs of a drowsy Polish town. Those who still had some strength left supported their weaker brethren. Women carried babies in their arms. Those who stepped out of line were shot by the guards. After about half-hour of trudging, we were greeted by Jewish laborers, setting out for another day of slavery.

"*Sholem aleichem!*" they said in Yiddish. "Have no fear, you've arrived at the ghetto of Rzeszow."

## *Chapter 4*
# GHETTO

*I*N THE RZESZOW GHETTO we were housed in a block of half-ruined buildings: shattered windows patched up here and there with wet cardboard, floors strewn with filthy feathers in vacant apartments. We were crammed in, four or five families to a room, with the toughest immediately grabbing the corners for their own. We, an old worn-out man, two women, and a child, were left with the open space in the middle, which was soon encroached upon from all sides as people claimed more territory by spreading out their blankets on the floor and laying their children down for the night. The only bed I could offer Tommy was my wet overcoat, but still he fell asleep in an instant. We huddled down beside him, watching over him anxiously in the freezing cold. There was nothing to do but wait until morning.

At first light we were ordered by the Judenrat to assemble in the main square for registration. Roommates of ours who knew some of the ghetto inmates leaked the news to us that two weeks earlier, a transport of some three thousand children had been shipped out of Rzeszow. Only a few had not been listed for deportation, including the children of the Judenrat chairman, the doctor, and the cobbler who mended the Gestapo officers' boots. Some other children, however, had been hidden and still survived.

Leaving our own children in our newfound "lodgings," we lined up in the square, where we were watched over by a man neatly dressed in a dark suit. His armband identified him as the chairman of the Judenrat. I thought I knew him, so when he reached our rank, I ventured to speak his name: "Mr. Serog?"

He paused, but it was clear he didn't recognize me, so I added, "It's Hilde Huppert, from Teschen."

"Hilde, the beauty with the long braids! How you've changed. And this must be Mr. Huppert, good day to you, sir. Can I be of help in any way?"

"My little boy, Tommy. I had to leave him in our room, and they say…"

"So you heard already. Don't worry. I have no news of any further transports. Just go ahead and register for employment. I'll see you later, I have to hurry now."

Once registered, anyone with any kind of craft skills, including Aunt Jenny and myself, was herded into the ghetto workshops: vast sheds with huge windows and hundreds of workers stooped over their benches. As we entered, the workers glanced up at the newcomers, but didn't dare say a word in the presence of their German overseers. The works manager relegated us to the different sections: tailors' shop, cobblers' shop, carpenters' shop, furriers, handicrafts, and so forth. Jenny and I were assigned to knit work, where a seemingly friendly woman of ample dimensions eased herself along her bench to make room for us. We were each tossed a bundle of ragged sweaters by the Jewish foreman. "Unravel all this, save the wool carefully, and then knit men's mittens. Do a good job and work fast. Your minimum quota is one pair a day. It's cold for the soldiers out there at the front."

All this was barked out in Polish, but as he leaned over us, he added in a whispered Yiddish, "May they all freeze to death: hands, feet, and you know what."

OUR SHIFT was from 7:00 A.M. to 8:30 P.M., with a bowl of soup and a slice of bread for "lunch." Jenny and I wolfed our own portions, setting aside a little of the bread for Sigmund and Tommy. I noticed that quite a number of the old hands didn't touch this ghastly gruel but instead spread napkins on the table and began taking out food they had brought from home. It was hard for me to keep my eyes off the woman opposite me who was gorging herself on a luscious ripe pear.

Returning "home" exhausted, we found that we had a little more living space. Some of our roommates had found better quarters through contacts with their friends in the ghetto, so now we, too, had a corner to ourselves. Sigmund and Tommy were seated on a blanket by the cardboard-paned window, both looking cleaned up and well fed. My father-in-law explained that the chairman of the Judenrat had taken them to his home, where they had been treated to a bath and a hot meal that his wife had prepared.

"As we were leaving," Sigmund added, "Mrs. Serog gave me this blanket and a whole loaf of bread. May the Lord bless her for her charity."

"Sigmund! Since when do you talk like that?" My secular father-in-law ignored my interjection.

"You should have seen Tommy and me at table once we were cleaned up. I'm only sorry that the two of you couldn't have been with us."

It was Mr. Serog who arranged employment for Sigmund at the offices of the Judenrat. And employment meant survival.

That evening I wrote to Mrs. Kenerova, informing her that we were now in the Rzeszow Ghetto and begging Mama to send us some cash that Sigmund had hidden in one of the books he left behind in Ivonitch. "We are still alive, still together, still with hope in our hearts," I wrote. The letter was mailed by a man who worked outside the ghetto and who risked his life by sending it.

The following morning, while we were busy unraveling and knitting, a stout woman began to talk: "My husband was a plasterer; he worked in the Aryan area of town, so for a few weeks he would come home with potatoes he'd bought from Polish peasants. Then one of the German guards searches his bag and reports on him; they take him to the Gestapo, and I haven't seen him since."

She also had a lot to tell about the recent *Aktion:* "We were all here in the workshops, only the kids and the old folks were left at home. All of a sudden the whole ghetto was flooded with German soldiers and Polish police. They went from room to room raking in the children and the old people, driving them into the square near the gate. The kids, screaming for their parents, were loaded into cattle cars at the railway station. Back home from work, all we found were empty, silent rooms, and little jackets still hanging on the walls: they took them away in a freezing December without any coats. I was lucky – on that day my daughter was here with me at work."

"Where did they take the children?" I couldn't help blurting out.

"You're still very naive, Mrs. Hilde. Look around you, don't you realize where you are? Whose woolens do you think we're unraveling? True, they've been laundered before we get them, but that's just to remove the bloodstains. You don't believe me, do you? Well, listen: About a couple of months ago they deported something like twenty thousand Jews from Rzeszow; they were loaded onto trains and sent off East. Ever heard of Auschwitz? That's it, then. A few weeks later we start getting shipments of clothes, knapsacks, suitcases. Some of us here even recognized the belongings of our relatives who'd been sent off on that transport. Now do you realize where this wool we're working on comes from?"

Suddenly it became silent, a sign that the German overseer was in the workshop. Only the clicking of knitting needles could be heard as all the women labored diligently, darting a furtive glance now and then at the blond young man who paced his measured way between the workbenches.

A pistol shot, a windowpane shattered, and the knitting needles dropped from my nerveless fingers. A heavy treading on my toes from the woman next to me was a warning sign, so I swiftly went on knitting. After a short, slightly hysterical laugh, the overseer quit our area and went on to the next shed.

"He likes to scare people," my workmate was muttering. "He hit that clock on the window sill, right behind Rebecca."

Our overseer, so it would seem, suffered from claustrophobia. He insisted that all doors be left open at all times. One evening the workshops suffered a power failure, and since the electrician didn't rush to fix the fuses, we enjoyed a welcome break. Someone asked for a song in honor of the newcomers, and a girl volunteered. The darkened shed became filled with the plaintive sound of Jewish folksongs, soon echoed by the women in the other workshops close by. One of the girls (the daughter of the Jewish clerk in charge of the warehouses, who was on good terms with the German overseer) shut the door and leaned against it so that we shouldn't be disturbed. As we began to enjoy the singing, there came a knocking on the door.

"Go away, leave us alone," the girl shouted, still leaning against the door.

By now it wasn't knocking but pounding, and we could recognize the voice of the overseer screeching outside. The girl just managed to slip back to her place before the door burst open and the lights came back on.

"Who shut that door?" the overseer bellowed as he stood on the threshold.

Without a word, we were back to our needles, knitting away furiously.

"I demand absolute silence. I give you exactly one minute. If by that time the culprit does not present herself, you will all get fifty lashes." (He enjoyed beating women's bottoms.)

A minute, according to the overseer's gold watch, was soon over. A middle-aged woman made her way to the center of the shed, raised her skirt, and bent over the bench. At that point, her daughter, who worked in our group, confronted the overseer.

"Don't whip my mama, whip me."

Shoving her mother aside, she bent over the bench, baring her backside to the somewhat startled supervisor.

"Get up girl," he snarled after a moment, "there'll be no whippings today. Let me take a look at you. Well, quite a pretty one. But I want the culprit! You have three minutes or else I will shoot three of you. You know you can depend on my word."

We were well aware of that. The minutes ticked by one after the other, and the girl who had actually shut the door said nothing. So it was I who spoke almost at the last second.

"I shut the door."

I could hear Jenny whispering, "Hilde, think of Tommy!" I could also sense forty-nine pairs of eyes staring at me.

"You?" the blond man questioned me.

"I beg your pardon for it," I replied in my best, polite German.

"You could never reach that door: at least twenty women block your way." He pondered for a moment. "So we have two heroines today. What's your name?"

"Hilde Huppert, Herr Overseer."

"Hilde Huppert. I have noted the name. Take care that I don't catch you out in another lie. I hate liars. And this lot…you've had enough time off. Get back to work and make sure that whoever shut that door is in my office first thing tomorrow morning. I'm curious to meet her!"

Once the overseer had gone, we quickly summoned the girl's father from his post in the warehouses. At first he seemed terrified, and then reassuring that he could sort the whole thing out with the overseer over a couple of drinks.

"I'll find him some expensive gift…He'll pardon her."

The girl reported to the overseer the following morning; he gave her a verbal reprimand and sent her back to her workbench.

In addition to the blond overseer, there was a German officer in charge who was responsible for the workforce. The woman next to me whispered that sometimes he showed sympathy for the Jews: "But you never can tell. Not long ago they searched the ghetto. Anyone absent from work, for whatever reason, was to be shot. In one building the Gestapo found about ten Jewish mothers who had stayed home to look after their sick children. They ordered them out into the courtyard and began to open fire. When this officer heard the shooting and saw what was going on, he was down there within a moment, asking them to cut it out. 'Who gave you orders to kill off my laborers? These women were working the nightshift; they've got a day off.' He managed to save six women, but that same night he got so drunk that he beat the living daylight out of one of the Jewish workers."

Every morning a group of workers was assigned to the communal kitchen. Most of the women were envious of this assignment because it gave them a chance of secretly filling an ever-hungry stomach. One woman was unlucky enough to be caught in the act of hiding away a yellow turnip (the basic commodity of ghetto soup) by the blond overseer, who happened to find her on one of his unexpected prowls. He shot her, inflicting a serious wound, and she was rushed to the infirmary by a few of her coworkers.

"Missed again," he muttered as he returned his pistol to its holster and marched out of the kitchen. Back in his office he issued an order that the "thief" be eliminated. On arriving at the infirmary, the Gestapo policeman found three weeping children at the injured woman's bedside, pleading to him to save their mother's life. After a moment's hesitation he ordered everyone out of the room. Then a shot was heard. "Robbery" had been punished to the full severity of the law.

Returning from the workshop one evening I found Sigmund collapsed on his mattress, apparently from a severe heart attack. At my urgent plea, the ghetto doctor, Dr. Hauptmann, came at once. Dr. Hauptmann was as jovial as he could be with the elderly patient. He gave him an injection, and then drew me aside, speaking in an undertone:

"I'll leave you a few injections; you know how to use them, don't you?"

"Of course," I replied, even though I doubted my ability.

"I'll stop by tomorrow evening. He should get as much rest as possible. What could really be of help would be a good bowl of chicken soup, but who can afford that nowadays?"

"Doctor Hauptmann, all I have is this small leather briefcase. We're new here in the ghetto and have no money so far."

"Pay me when you can," he said, rejecting the gift. "I accept money only from those who have it. You look as if you're in need of a tonic yourself. Remind me to give you something next time I come."

One day there was near panic in the workshops. Word had gotten out that the German Kommandant was planning a check up to weed out the weakest and the elderly who weren't fulfilling their quotas. Many of the elderly women dressed themselves up as best they could and wore lipstick in a desperate attempt to seem a little younger.

As the Kommandant made his way from one shed to another, eyeing both men and women alike, a grim smile came to his lips: "What goes on ladies? You all seem to be ready for a masked ball!"

The Kommandant seemed to show a special interest in the new arrivals, and when he reached our bench, he inquired about me, upon which the blond overseer relayed the incident of the closed door. The Kommandant then asked me where I had lived before the war. When I told him I had lived in Teschen in Silesia, he recalled that the chairman of the Judenrat was from the same town. As a result, after a meeting between the Kommandant and Mr. Serog, I was appointed liaison between the German overseer and the Jewish workers.

Later, when all the firewood in the ghetto had been used up I suggested the idea of mounting "clean-up operations" in abandoned buildings that still contained bits and pieces of broken furniture. The officer in charge bought the idea, ordering the Judenrat to provide the necessary workforce. This scheme created several new jobs, and as a result, quite a few new permits for ghetto residence. Only the families of the employed were permitted to remain within the ghetto.

After some days of this office work, I was summoned back to the knitting shed. My former bench mate seemed very upset.

"They've arrested my cousin Joseph," she sobbed.

Her cousin Joseph Theh, she explained, was a Judenrat policeman; he had held three-monthly passes because he was often sent out of the ghetto on Judenrat business.

"Yesterday," she was choking on her words, "he went to renew his pass and was told to come back tomorrow. And today they arrested him outside the ghetto because his pass had expired. They have taken him to the Gestapo at Kreisburg: That's a place you get to, God help us, but never leave. My poor Joseph. His mother and father were shot down in the last *Aktion*. Maybe you can do something? Talk to someone."

I appealed to my boss, the German officer in charge.

"You haven't been here long, have you? Otherwise you wouldn't be asking me to do the impossible."

"But you have saved..."

"Don't argue with me! That was a different matter. Kreisburg makes its own laws; I'm not prepared to stick my neck out there."

That evening I went to see Mr. Serog. He had heard about what had happened and was already looking for someone to replace Joseph Theh. When I asked him why he didn't apply personally to the Gestapo and explain the matter, he looked at me as if uncertain I was in my right mind.

"My dear Hilde! I go to the Gestapo only when called. I write down my orders; I reply 'Yes sir,' 'No sir,' 'At your command sir,' and ask no questions. Short answers. I would never dream of arguing, or bargaining."

Two days after Joseph Theh was arrested, there was a newly appointed Judenrat policeman going in and out of the ghetto with a three-month pass.

One day, when I was in the midst of allotting the work quotas, a young girl came into the office and whispered to me that there was a Polish woman waiting for me at the gates to the ghetto. After begging a moment from the officer in charge, I rushed out to the gates where a Judenrat policeman agreed to let me peek through the spy-hatch. I was overcome with joy to see our former landlady from Ivonitch. She had received my letter and had been sent on this mission to Rzeszow by Mama. Mrs. Kenerova was pointing to a small bundle she held wrapped up in a kerchief. I appealed for help from the Judenrat policeman, but he was hesitant, afraid of the German guards around the gate. On a sudden impulse, Mrs. Kenerova hurled the package over the fence and hurried away. Since no one seemed to have noticed, I snatched it up and rushed back to the workshops.

The package contained a sweater, a pair of sandals (I had concealed a precious diamond in one of its heels), and a letter from Mama. She wrote that she and Ruthy were in good health and were being well taken care of by Mrs. Kenerova. However she added that the Germans had recently begun house-to-house searches for young men dodging the forced-labor call-up and that this could lead to Ruthy and herself being discovered. She also wrote that

Marcus was still in the labor camp near Rymanov, but that there were rumors that the camp was scheduled to be dismantled. We managed to sell the diamond through a deal with a laborer with an outside work permit, who smuggled food back into the ghetto for us. The diamond saved our lives: for six more weeks we were able to conquer our hunger.

THE WINTER of 1943 was harsh. We worked in constant fear of the transports, doing our best to simply hang on. One day I was informed that there was a telegram for me at the Judenrat offices. I hurried there to find it was from Mrs. Kenerova's son, Juzek. It read simply, "Your passports are at the central post office in Krosno."

Later on I learned that Juzek had just happened to be in the post office when the postmaster recognized him and casually remarked, "By the way, I've got some English documents here addressed to those Jews who used to board at your mother's place. They've been lying around here for a couple of weeks with no claimers. I suppose I'll just have to mark them return to sender."

Guessing that the papers would likely be useful to us, Juzek persuaded him to hold them for a bit longer, and after consulting with his mother, sent me his telegram.

I bribed a Polish wagoner, a daily visitor to the ghetto, to cable my address to the Krosno postmaster, and sure enough, a registered package arrived a few days later containing immigration certificates to Palestine for Tommy and myself. Yet it was a kind of cold comfort: There were only two entry permits. There were four of us. (Soon after this, a new edict was issued forbidding Jews to use the mail. Even letters sent under Red Cross auspices failed to arrive. *Just suppose those certificates had been sent a few days late; just suppose Mrs. Kenerova's son hadn't chanced to visit the Krosno post office...just suppose...*)

That same evening I consulted with Mr. Serog and told him

of my intention to write to the Gestapo to request permission to emigrate on the basis of my Palestine certificates. The chairman expressed doubts about the idea, fearing that it might give the authorities an excuse to arrest me. I explained that the documents had passed through censorship so that the Gestapo must surely know about them.

"If they'd wanted to arrest us, they'd have done it by now," I said. As he still seemed reluctant, I threw a question at him. "Supposing you had such entry permits, wouldn't you appeal to the Gestapo?"

"That's another matter. All right. Write out your request, I'll pass it on."

Gestapo headquarters promptly reacted with an official letter informing us that Tommy and I were listed for exchange against German citizens held by the Allied Powers, and that we would just have to await our turn.

AT THE END of January 1943 the workforce from the Rymanov labor camp was transferred to the Rzeszow Ghetto. Among them was my brother-in-law Marcus. The newcomers were placed in our workshops, and Marcus moved in with us.

Marcus hardly ever spoke a word, except when setting out for work in the morning when he would mutter a bitter, "One more day." On returning in the evening he would mumble, "And Rega?"

There was no answer to this, and he really didn't expect one. He would eat with us ravenously, but in silence. Only when I mentioned his daughter would his blank eyes light up with a flicker of momentary interest, "Ruthy...yes...Ruthy." (That was all.)

FEBRUARY 1943: On our way to work in the biting cold we saw a heavy truck pulling up outside the ghetto gates and some twenty gaunt and tattered men dragging themselves out the back. I stopped for a moment to watch the grim scene, but the woman behind me was nudging me forward.

"Get a move on Hilde, you're only asking for trouble."

Later, one of the women in the workshop, who had been there much longer than I, explained. "They're from the steelworks at Stalowswola, not far from here. They work them eighteen hours a day, and the overseers make quite sure that the work quotas are filled. Hard labor and poor food take their toll – every so often they trade in these wrecks for healthier manpower."

There was a manhunt that day throughout the entire ghetto. The S.S. were searching for able-bodied younger men to be sent to the steelworks. A room was found for the pitiful invalids who had been sent back from Stalowswola. We collected food and clothing for them, cared for them as best we could. At this time we were unaware that they carried the germs of what destined to wreak havoc in the ghetto: typhus.

TWO DAYS LATER we heard shooting from the direction of our homes.

"What's going on? Who're they shooting now?"

Our voices were on the verge of panic, but we were forbidden to leave work before the end of our shift. After about fifteen minutes we could see (from the workshop windows) the S.S. leaving the ghetto.

*I had left Tommy at "home." Would I ever see him again?*

I was frantic with worry when (as we eventually left work) we found the streets deserted. There were bloodstains and the traces of bodies having been dragged away. It was then we saw the handcarts and the flashing torches, and the men loading the corpses. Here and there we could hear moaning and groaning; apparently not all had been killed. As I approached, I saw with a flicker of relief that they were all adults: the sick and maimed from the steelworks.

I walked away, and then began to run through the darkness. I was no longer frantic – I was terrified. The trembling only stopped when I was cradling Tommy in my arms. His lean face was ashen with fear. I tried to calm him, but I couldn't find the words.

When Sigmund returned from his work at the Judenrat, he was able to fill in the details: A six-man S.S. unit had made its way into the ghetto demanding to see the laborers released from Stalowswola. The human skeletons were ordered up off their mattresses and commanded to run around in the square outside. The weakest were forced up by kicks and blows.

"Come on men, show a leg!" (The sergeant was screaming at them.) They staggered slowly around the courtyard in a pitiful, grotesque spectacle. The S.S. were roaring with laughter, exchanging bets about which of the victims was the funniest, which would last the longest, which would be the first to fall. They soon got bored with the show and opened fire on the creatures, who began to scuttle for safety. Once they had shot them all, the S.S. retreated.

I LIVED IN THE GHETTO OF RZESZOW for a total of seven months…if you can describe such terror-filled existence as "living." Hardly a day or night passed without us witnessing some act of brutality. Many of our friends and neighbors were on the brink of suicide, preferring death to a life dominated by fear. It was different for Tommy and me: we still had a spark of hope.

On returning from work one evening, Jenny and I found a cheerful fire blazing in the hearth, the entire room scrubbed spick-and-span, and a hot meal on the rickety table. Glancing around, I was astonished to see both Mama and Ruthy. After much hugging and kissing we were given our orders: "Sit down and eat. You must be starving and exhausted."

Dearest Mama, to her I was still a little girl to be cared for. But after all this time of being responsible for our tiny family, it was a relief to have someone with whom to share the burden. We had been eating for a while when she told her story. The Germans had been conducting exhaustive searches, and Mrs. Kenerova had been getting scared.

"She never told us to leave, but I could tell that it was time to go.

I thanked her for all she had done for us; we embraced, she made a sign of a cross, blessing me. What would Papa Zelig, may he rest in peace, have said about that?"

"He would have accepted the blessing. Papa was a wise man."

"I know, Hildeleh. So I blessed them in return. Mrs. Kenerova, Juzek, and Hella. Those two are very fond of each other, they're talking about getting married."

Mama and Ruthy had taken a small suitcase and trudged through the hills for several days, sleeping overnight by the wayside and once in a farmer's woodshed.

"Ruthy was wonderful. She really had a good time, didn't you, Ruthy?"

"We walked through the fields, we saw the sky, but then my feet began to hurt and I was crying. Granny didn't tell you that bit."

"My feet hurt, too," Mama consoled her, "but in the end we got here, we found your Papa, and Grandpa Sigmund, Aunt Hilde, Aunt Jenny, and Tommy...and everyone."

"Not everyone." Ruthy held back her tears. "Not Mama."

Ruthy slunk off into a corner to sit with Tommy, who was listening attentively to everything Mama was saying: "Here in Rzeszow I hung around outside the gates to the ghetto, and when it started to get dark and the workers were coming back, we managed to mingle with one of the groups and get inside."

Later, Mama whispered to me, "I've seen Marcus. He doesn't say very much, but Ruthy and I are both certain that he's glad we came."

I offered to arrange a job for Mama in the workshops, but she rejected it: "I'll just stay here in the room and care for my grandchildren and for the other children of the working women." Then she added a decisive afterthought. "I have no wish to work for the Germans."

"Mama," I pleaded with her, "you're new here, you don't understand the way things are. If you don't have a work permit, you don't get any food rations, and if they find you in one of the house-to-house searches, you'll be sent away."

"So let them find me." Mama seemed to take my warnings quite calmly. "Let them send me away. In the meantime someone has to look after the children."

Very soon, dear Mama had made many friends and acquaintances in the ghetto, and all the kids were calling her Granny.

When the officer in charge was transferred to the front, a new overseer was appointed to the workshops. On his very first day he conducted a review of all manpower and laid off all the elderly, including Aunt Jenny, who was the best knitting woman in the shed. It was his habit to prowl through the workshops during our scanty lunch break and check our food for smuggled goods. After work we had to stand in line for lengthy head counts and to witness the daily punishments. There were whippings every evening: twenty, twenty-five lashes, fifty, seventy-five, and occasionally even graver penalties. During one of his surprise raids into the ghetto, our new Kommandant discovered a secret cellar in which some thirty local dignitaries lived in hiding. Summoning reinforcements, he had the building surrounded and its underground residents ordered to come out with their hands up. When they did so, the soldiers started shooting.

There were about two hundred workers who were let out of the ghetto every day for outside work. They were the "lucky ones," the envy of all the inmates, for they were conscripted for "vital" tasks and could thus obtain precious items of food. The best jobs were to be found at Rzeszow railway station. It was there that the Judenrat would dispatch a squad of lawyers, doctors, and the fairly wealthy, who would compete with one another for the privilege of working as a platform porter. Rumor had it in the ghetto that these men were loaded with valuables that they would conceal on themselves. Apparently, such rumors reached the Kommandant. One evening he sealed the gates with a Gestapo unit, and when the railway workers returned from their shift, they were ordered to line up and strip. The Gestapo went through the clothes and then conducted body searches, but little of value was found. Frustrated, the Kommandant marched off, throwing an order over his shoulder: "What are you waiting for? Finish them off."

ONE OF THE HARSHEST of the new edicts was that the workers were required to live in the workshop compound away from their families, the aim being to separate the workforce from the unemployed. Every evening one could see children and their mothers clustered along the barbed-wire fence, which now divided the workshop area from the ghetto proper. An overseer would prowl up and down, chasing the kids away from their mothers on the other side of the wire. At this point I resigned from my job in order to remain with my family. The Kommandant had no problem finding a replacement.

Soon after, Sigmund retuned from the Judenrat bearing bad news. The Cracow Ghetto had been liquidated; only those holding "vital" jobs had been spared.

"You get back to work, Hilde!" Sigmund was adamant. "Don't argue with me. You get back to the workshops tomorrow."

TYPHUS BROKE OUT in the ghetto: more and more cases were discovered every day. We feared that if the Germans found out about the epidemic, they would set fire to the entire area, houses and inhabitants alike. The elderly and infirm were the main victims of the disease. Most of the workers were not affected, and so the Judenrat was able to conceal the crisis from the German authorities. Deaths were reported as due either to "natural causes" or "old age." The women volunteered to nurse the sick, the men to bury the dead. One of these volunteer nurses was Aunt Jenny, who

staggered home one evening with a raging fever. After only a brief
examination, Doctor Hauptmann warned me: "It's typhus. Try to
keep away from her."

I didn't. I stayed beside her, and Mama kept the children at a
distance. Jenny was delirious. As I wiped her forehead with a damp
cloth, I felt a sudden dizziness and a stinging in my eyes. When I
was certain no one was watching, I took my temperature: it was an
ominous 38.9° C (102° F).

"No!" I cried inwardly, refusing to give in, "It's just a chill."
How could I fall sick with a room full of little kids and strangers
anxiously staring at me and Jenny lying helpless at my feet? As I
hastily swallowed an aspirin, I tried to convince myself, "It's just
a chill, Hilde. You've had worse than that. This is no time for self-
indulgence." Thus persuaded, I continued to sit at Jenny's side.

The next day I couldn't even struggle up from my mattress. I
vaguely glimpsed Mama offering me a glass of tea and stroking
my feverish forehead before I passed out again. When I regained
consciousness, Jenny's mattress was empty. Seeing the unspoken
question in my eyes, Mama reassured me that Aunt Jenny had been
taken to the infirmary and would feel much better now.

True, Aunt Jenny was already in another place, another world
in which all was said to be good and well. My fever had now
reached 41.5° C (106.7° F) and crisis was close at hand. Now and
then I could see Mama as if in the mist, stooping over me with a
cool spoon of something I was supposed to swallow. I was so weak
by now that I found it hard even to sip the medicine; it was only
the sight of those soft, entreating eyes of my exhausted mother
that gave me the strength to do so. I continued to become weaker
and weaker all the time. I had the feeling that one long, endless
sleep was taking over, which would carry me off to the next world.
I was awakened by shouts. "Why can't you let me sleep?" I pleaded
as I opened my eyes. Mama had risked the lives of the children
by bringing them to me and exposing them to the disease. She

made Tommy and Ruthy swear not to let me die. I could hear their voices as if through a fog: "Mama, Mama, don't go away, don't leave us…Mama, don't die!"

"Why can't you leave me alone? All I want is to sleep." Again I closed my eyes, but Tommy and Ruthy were still yelling at me, weeping, refusing to leave me alone. At the same time, Mama, who had rushed to summon Dr. Hauptmann, was screaming at the doctor, "My daughter is dying! You have to save her…you must!"

The doctor was supported by two youngsters as he dragged himself out of his own sickbed to visit mine. After a brief pat of Tommy's head, Dr. Hauptmann got down to business: his diagnosis was that the situation was extremely grave. After a long moment of consideration, he muttered that treating me might be a waste of an expensive injection. Nevertheless he opened his bag and took out the needle. When Mama asked him about the chances, he whispered to her, "If you believe in God, pray to Him. He's the only one who can help now."

After the injection I slept soundly. The doctor, exhausted from his efforts, took a lengthy rest at our place before returning to his own room and bed. This time, too, he refused any payment.

Dr. Hauptmann had become infected by his own patients' typhus. The old warrior, who fought diseases with aspirin and encouraging words, was finally vanquished. He was dead within a few days.

NOW AND THEN a miracle occurs in our world, and one of these happened to me: The crisis passed, the fever decreased, the disease was cured. As I laid recuperating on my mattress, I was visited by a young rabbi who served as spiritual leader of the ghetto during the typhus epidemic. He was also regarded as something of a *Ba'al Shem*, or visionary. After looking at me and blessing me he turned to Mama and told her, "Be not afraid for your daughter. Last night I saw her in my dream walking throughout the Land of Israel."

Mama questioned how he could possibly know this. He replied simply, "I am certain. I have seen it with my own eyes."

Then he left.

When the children brought me a couple of wildflowers they had picked next to the barbed-wire fence, Tommy told me in all seriousness that it was he who had brought me back from "over there."

Once I was allowed to get up off my mattress, I was so weak that I had to learn to walk all over again. During my illness I had lost over twenty pounds.

Somewhat recovered, I made my way to the Judenrat to inquire about any news regarding our exit permits. After receiving an unsatisfying answer from the clerk in charge, I realized nothing had been done. I now had to consider my next move: I didn't dare apply to the Gestapo headquarters, and Jews were not allowed to approach Gestapo officers on the streets of the ghetto. I had to find another way.

Recuperating from an illness as severe as mine meant getting a lot of fresh air, so I spent a great deal of time outdoors. One day, while I was sipping a glass of water with Tommy at my side, watching over me with love and concern, we suddenly heard the cry "Gestapo!" ringing out and echoing around all the street corners. Within the blink of an eye, all the streets and courtyards were empty. I tried to get up, but my legs were weak; Tommy gently supported me, knowing that I was in pain.

"It's all right Mama. Sit down again, I'll take care of you." Some way off we could see the Gestapo Kommandant and the Judenrat chairman accompanied by armed soldiers. I had an inexplicable impulse to send Tommy to speak with the German officer. I gave Tommy hurried instructions, which he repeated to me word for word.

"Now go to them, and don't show them you're scared."

Seven-year-old Tommy marched up with his short steps to the

approaching officials and was greeted by glances of surprise from both Gestapo and Judenrat alike. Addressing them in faultless German he recited: "My name is Thomas Huppert. The woman over there," he pointed at me, "is my mother. We are both British subjects and have immigration certificates to Palestine. Herr Kommandant, can you tell us when we will be allowed to go? I miss my Daddy." After staring for a moment at the little Tommy, the Gestapo officer turned to Mr. Serog.

"Huppert? I seem to know the name."

"*Natuerlich Herr Kommandant*," the Judenrat chairman hastened to reply. "The moment we received the documents they were sent to you for review."

"True, true. Well my lad, you'll have to tell your mama to be a little patient. We have much to do you know, but you won't be forgotten." Tommy ran back, radiant, to tell me the good news. After we had both calmed down a bit, I reminded him that he had forgotten to say thank you and goodbye.

"Do you want me to run back and do that?" my boy asked me with a mischievous glint in his eye.

"Never!" I cried out, hugging him close.

That same day, three Jewish policemen were arrested in the ghetto by a unit of the S.S. They were instructed to stand against a wall and were shot. No charges had been filed against them. The three simply knew too much about the tortures conducted in the Gestapo dungeons, and the Germans preferred to leave no witnesses.

It took several days before a Jewish policeman entered our room and requested that Tommy and I accompany him to the Gestapo headquarters at Kreisburg.

"Nothing to worry about. They said they just want a little talk with you and then you'll be returned to the ghetto."

Despite the fact that his words seemed to soothe my family's fears, I parted from them with the uneasy feeling I might never see my relatives again. As we trudged through the ghetto streets, I could sense the anxious glances, I could hear the whispers…*Kreisburg.*

At the ghetto gates our escort presented our papers to the German guards; the gates were opened and we were out. It was a wonderful feeling to be outside of the barbed-wire, to see people walking freely in the streets, peering into shop windows, talking to one another loudly instead of in hushed tones. Some passersby noticed my white armband with its Star of David. There were those who looked on it with compassion, those who seemed indifferent, and those who regarded it with open hatred. On arrival at the Kreisburg offices we were offered a place to sit down, and our police escort was told to return within the hour. This seemed to be quite encouraging. As we waited, I watched the clerks hurrying back and forth, the armed guards with their measured gait, and the Gestapo with their aura of power and fear. After some time, we were summoned into one of the offices. An official was peering at our documents, and afterwards at us.

"Hilde and Thomas Huppert?"

"Yes, sir," I replied.

"Well, it would seem at long last that the British are showing some interest in you. They are willing to exchange you for some German citizens they are holding in captivity. First of all, we'll send you to Germany for a little recuperation. We would like the whole world to know that we treat our hostages well. After that, you'll have a passage through Istanbul to Palestine. Any questions?"

"Could I take my niece with me? She's only seven, the same age as Tommy here."

The Gestapo officer seemed to listen patiently before replying: "I'm sorry, madam. As far as we are concerned you could all go, it is the British who make the problems. Two certificates – two Jews. Were those all the questions?"

There was nothing more to ask, so I nodded my head.

"So be ready this evening, and don't take too much luggage."

I rose from my seat with a heavy heart: I had not succeeded in saving Ruthy.

"You may remove your armband," the officer said.

"If you don't mind, I'll keep it on until I leave the ghetto."

The news that I had actually returned from Kreisburg and was actually going to Palestine spread throughout the ghetto like wildfire. I was besieged by people giving me letters to relatives abroad, all of them bearing the same message: "Save us. Get us passports."

Mama and Sigmund rejoiced in our good fortune, but Ruthy clung to me, and I had the feeling I was abandoning her. Marcus remained secluded in his own world of nightmares. When I tried to explain to him that I was leaving, his only reaction was to nod and ask, "And Rega?"

The police knocked on the door at four in the morning. I was already dressed, I woke Tommy, Mama swiftly prepared him something hot to drink.

I hugged Mother, kissed Sigmund, stroked a sleeping Ruthy, and pressed the silent hand of Marcus. Then we were out into the reluctant dawn of the ghetto. My mother stood at the window of the half-ruined building, waving to me in what she knew would be a last goodbye.

A black horse-drawn carriage awaited us at the ghetto gates with a Gestapo officer on board gesturing at us to clamber in. Once we were inside the coach, Tommy was clutching me fiercely. "To the railway station," I heard the officer command the coachman.

We had a reserved compartment on the train. Our Gestapo escort ignored us throughout the entire journey. It was only upon our arrival in Cracow that he glanced at us with the cryptic comment, "Consider yourselves lucky." The officer called up a horse-drawn cab and gave its driver our new destination: Monte Lupe.

## Chapter 5
## PRISON

A T FIRST I DIDN'T REALIZE where they had brought us, but soon enough the high walls, the prison guards, and, of course, the cells, made it quite clear that our period of "recuperation" was to be spent in another prison. Frightened at the thought, I warned Tommy: "Even if they give you an order, tell them you're staying with Mama!" Our escort handed us over for registration to the duty officer with the curt comment, "Hostages bound for Palestine." Then he departed without a further word. It seemed as if they were really intending to exchange us. The duty officer was on the phone, seemingly resenting the orders he was being given.

"What do you mean 'humane treatment'? Don't we all know what goes on, on the other side?"

As he slammed down the phone he barked at us, "Move along, both of you."

And so the two of us were marched off to the cells.

The place was crowded with women and children, and almost before the door was shut and locked, we were surrounded by a barrage of questions.

"What ghetto are you from?" "What passports have you got?" "Do you have any food?" "Any cigarettes?"

On being told that we held certificates for Palestine and would soon be exchanged, there was a chorus of hollow laughter. They also had husbands in Palestine; they also had been given promises; and they had been here in Monte Lupe prison for weeks on end. Most of them came from the Tarnow Ghetto and had escaped the last *Aktion* by hiding in cellars and in attics.

"At first," one of the women told us, "there were some thirty or forty thousand people in the ghetto. When we left, there were only four thousand. All the rest had been taken on the transports."

That night we could hear screams and cries for help. The more experienced of our cellmates shrugged this off as a regular nightly ritual. The following morning, through the crack in the boarded-up window, I could glimpse prisoners crawling up a coal heap in the courtyard. They were on their elbows and knees, being whipped by the Gestapo as they made their miserable way to the top. If one of them fainted, he was doused with a bucket of water and then "encouraged" to continue. Later they transferred Tommy and me to a mass cell, reserved for the transports. There were a few men there crowded in with hundreds of women and children, all of whom had British passports or Palestine immigration certificates. Some of the women were from Palestine and had been in Europe visiting relatives when the war suddenly broke out, trapping them. Others, such as myself, held certificates obtained from their husbands in Palestine. We all sat on suitcases or parcels, none of us knew the destination of our transport.

Hundreds of inscriptions were scratched on the walls: "Tomorrow to Auschwitz"; "Rest at last"; "Tell my parents I was here"; "Live well"; "Farewell, no au revoir."

The signatures were both Jewish and Polish. Final greetings of slaughtered innocents, sentenced to death by no judge, by no court of law.

WE WAITED for two days. All the time I nursed a secret hope that this would prove to be our last confinement, that upon release from Monte Lupe I would find myself on the road to freedom – to my husband. A German official appeared and read out a long list of names. The lucky ones quickly assembled and followed him out. Tommy and I, as well as many of our companions, had not been called. There were several newcomers that evening from the Cracow Ghetto. Some had entry visas to the United States that had been sent by relatives. One of the women told me that the Germans didn't take these all that seriously. Out of ninety who had been imprisoned with her, there were only a few in the transport cell who had not been dispatched, one way or another. It took two days before the German official reappeared with another list. This time Tommy and I were on it.

As we marched through the corridors, I could hear the agonized appeals from cells on either side. Those voices, and the sight of the prisoners scrambling up the heaps of coal, were to be my last images of the Monte Lupe prison. Buses were waiting for us outside; the Germans were being surprisingly civil, checking the seating accommodations, asking if there were any complaints. The sight of a Gestapo officer handing out sandwiches for the journey almost made me vomit. At the railway station we were ushered on board a passenger train that made its way through Berlin and Hannover until we arrived at our destination. Here we were ordered to disembark and board trucks guarded by S.S. soldiers with fixed bayonets.

Once again our hearts sank: What had become of the sudden concern for our welfare? Why the S.S.? Did the Germans really suspect we might try to escape? What for? Weren't we on our way to Palestine?

It was at least an hour-long wait. Then there was a long journey through an uninhabited plain to a camp surrounded by both fence and watchtowers. Bare wooden shacks stood in rows, divided by barbed-wire barriers. Glancing around, trying to comprehend where we were, no one uttered a word. Tommy was pressing my hand, not daring to ask. We were met by several hundred people assembled in a vast area. These were the "lucky ones" who had been released a few days earlier from the transport cell. They were staring at us with curiosity, possibly partners in our despair, possibly gaining a certain comfort from our own disappointment. It was they who told us where we were: Bergen-Belsen.

## Chapter 6
## BERGEN-BELSEN

A LOUD-MOUTHED SERGEANT ordered us into one of the huts. Inside, half-starved prisoners dragged some straw mattresses onto two-tiered bunk beds; and then, between those ramshackle wooden frameworks, everyone began to talk. The air buzzed with unanswered questions: Where had they taken us? How long would they keep us here? How were we going to be treated? I stood there numb, listening to the babble, trying to form words into sentences and then make some sense of them. I could see Tommy sitting on our bed, shoes off, waiting. The prisoners brought us three blankets each, fondling them with their calloused hands, seemingly amazed that Jews should be given blankets at all. I snatched them away from the inmate who brought the blankets to our bunk. He was clinging to them like a madman, determined not to be deprived of their coarse comfort. Once I had grabbed the blankets he gazed at me for a moment before lowering a humiliated glance at his now-empty, bony hands. I wanted to shake out the blankets in the open air, but hesitated to leave the raucous company, which by its very hubbub seemed to give an illusion of friendship and security. Instead I shook them next to the bed, earning a torrent of curses from those around us. As I spread the blankets on the straw mattress, Tommy laid down at once on the lower bunk. I covered him up and kissed him: he had a smile on his face and was already asleep.

The prisoners were bringing in more stuff, setting up trestle tables and benches in the open space between the bunks. Then a German officer came in and demanded a German translator. After an uneasy moment or two, Erwin Zonderling, whom I had known as the owner of a textile factory at Bielitz, volunteered. He was ordered to dispatch a group of five to the kitchen to bring food; there were few who hesitated now. They soon returned with loaves of bread, packets of margarine, and even some white cheese. I woke Tommy and we sat down to eat. After this improvised meal, the future looked a little more promising: if they were in fact prepared to feed us so well, then perhaps...

We cleaned up and straightened things out as best we could. It was quite roomy. Even the children had beds.

Weeks went by and the food rations began to deteriorate. First to vanish were the cheese and the margarine; then there was less bread, and the noontime soup became more and more sparse and watery.

And so we spent the summer of 1943: long days in the hut or in the yard in the shadow of the wooden watchtower; head counts both morning and evening; ever-growing hunger, ever-dwindling hopes; cutbacks in the bread rations; the German Kommandant's pronouncements: "Those bastard English don't care about you!"

As we sat idle for hours on end, I would tell Tommy stories about our home in Teschen and about his Papa in Palestine. I would wax fervent as I described him, the tall and handsome man awaiting us in a land where the sun shined all the year round. Tommy would listen closely, but then ask to hear about the time when he was small and his Papa was still with us.

Certain hours were devoted to study. I would teach Tommy (in German) reading, writing, and arithmetic, as well as whatever geography I could muster. From there in Bergen-Belsen we would take off on fabulous imaginary journeys: floating down the Ganges, riding camels through the Sahara, climbing the snowcapped peak of Mount Kilimanjaro, but also to the top of the Empire State Building in New York. It was only when Tommy started asking questions that I realized what a meager education I had actually received.

During this period I began composing a few verses in which I tried to describe our hopes and dreams:

*My name is Thomas Huppert*
*They know me, young and old*
*I dwell in Bergen-Belsen*
*But Zion is my goal.*
*There's joy there, and the sun shines gold*
*There's laughter there, for young and old.*
*We await the answer to our prayer*
*But weeks and months go by*
*We are on the border of despair*
*And when we weaken, cry.*
*There's little food, the rain leaks in*
*The Germans scream: "Here must be clean!"*
*We rub and scrub, but all in vain*
*There's always mud, and always rain.*
*My song is over, yet I still*
*Pray to the Lord with all my will*
*That somehow we shall be set free*
*And when we finally do see*
*Our destination: Ankara*
*I'll shout aloud a great "Hurrah!"*
*My name is Thomas Huppert*
*They know me young and old*
*I dwell in Bergen-Belsen*
*But Zion is my goal.*

These words were an incantation, and Tommy would chant them with great devotion.

AUTUMN, 1943: a transport of some two hundred Jews arrive bearing passports from the Allied nations, most of them had previously been moved out of the Warsaw Ghetto. (The ghetto had been wiped out by the Germans after the heroic Jewish uprising in April 1943.) It was from them that we hear that some four hundred Jews bearing foreign passports had been shot to death in Warsaw's Pawiak prison. Life was also getting tough for those hiding in the Polish quarters. Many of the Poles were handing over Jews who had been hidden in their cellars because the Jews' money was running out.

After the Warsaw group, there was another transport from the Bochnia Ghetto. Some of them were on their way to Argentina. They firmly believed, as we had, that Bergen-Belsen would only be a short stopover. They had heard rumors that the Bochnia Ghetto was due to be eliminated in a matter of days.

The autumn rains turned the yard into a quagmire; icy winds howled between the huts setting the barbed-wire dancing. We could hear the sentry in the watchtower stamping his feet to keep himself warm, cursing the Jews and his own bitter fate.

I often had to wade through the mud out to the open latrine close to the barbed wire. The miserable diet and the constant tension led to stomach cramps and diarrhea. At first, I would try to hold back, just to avoid going out into the icy air under the ogling eyes of the guard; but then I would run for it, slipping and stumbling through the mud, barely reaching the stinking pit in time. In pain and helpless. I had no shame. I knew the sentry was watching. I could hear his laughter.

With the coming winter, we held a collection in our hut. Everyone was asked to donate whatever clothing he could spare, to be handed out to those who needed it more.

ROLL CALL WAS HELD OUTSIDE, morning and evening. We would stand for hours while rain (and later snow) lashed at us. Our shoes were falling apart and gave us little protection. Tommy had only one pair, and I had already been forced to cut them open because he had outgrown them. His toes stuck out into the mud and snow.

"Keep wiggling your toes!" I reminded him again and again, "otherwise you'll get frostbite."

The camp Kommandant of Bergen-Belsen was an Austrian *Obersturmbannfuehrer,* Adolf Haas. One day, during the morning head count, I whispered to Tommy to break ranks and to show the Herr Kommandant the state of his shoes. Adolf Haas seemed touched by this appeal from the almost barefoot little boy and was impressed by Tommy's perfect German, but declared he had no solution to the problem. It was then that Tommy played our trump card:

"We see new prisoners coming in every day; there must be lots of shoes left over after you dress them in pajamas and clogs, Herr Kommandant."

"Smart thinking!" Adolf Haas replied, and dispatched a trooper to the storerooms.

We were later summoned into his presence, where an entire sack load of boots and shoes were scattered onto the floor.

"Take first pick little boy! It was your idea!"

Tommy selected a pair of ugly rubber boots, which wouldn't have been my own choice, but it's probable that they saved him from contracting pneumonia. The remaining shoes were handed out to the other children in our hut.

IT WAS A LONG, LONG WINTER, but eventually spring came. Nature seldom disappoints. Even over Bergen-Belsen the sun shone brightly and our frozen limbs began to thaw. A warmth spread through our bodies and a ray of hope began to glimmer in our hearts.

During the spring of 1944, a German official visited us. Rumor had it that he belonged to the Foreign Office and carried a list of those destined to be released.

The rumor turned out to be true. "This transport," he declared, "will be sent to Bergau, near Dresden, for purposes of exchange."

We went wild with joy, but our spirits were soon dampened as he proceeded to read the names. All of them held American passports, there were no "Palestinians" on the list.

The transport was organized swiftly and efficiently, the official and his military escort hurried them along with shouted orders. The "Americans" became anxious; some of them, upon saying good-bye, expressed hope that they weren't being sent to Auschwitz.

Camp Kommandant Haas would visit our hut to inform us that arrangements for the exchange of "Palestinians" were continually being delayed. The Allies refused to accept us in exchange for German women and children who had been trapped in Palestine at the outbreak of war. As a result, the Germans became indifferent to our fate, treating us as an unwanted burden. Rations were systematically reduced, every few weeks we were shifted to even less inhabitable shacks. These moves were always sudden and unpredictable, giving rise to great anxiety.

Many of our group fell prey to various illnesses: Tommy alone contracted measles, smallpox, and several bouts of influenza and ear infections. There were no medicines. I fell ill several times but struggled to hold out. I knew my son needed me.

At night, lying on our narrow bunk with Tommy by my side, I would be haunted by visions of my mother, of Ruthy, of Sigmund, and of Marcus, whom we had left behind in the Rzcszow Ghetto. I could imagine them wondering why I hadn't yet fulfilled my promises to get them out. How could they possibly guess that we were stuck here in a concentration camp?

On one of his daily visits, Kommandant Haas informed us

that we were to be moved to better quarters, with better rations. True enough, we were shifted to what was known as the "Spanish Compound," a section of the camp reserved for Jewish prisoners of neutral nationality. Extra portions of bread and sunlight in the shacks gave us a renewed hope.

One of our new privileges was access to the shower blocks, which were situated near the camp gate. We, who had so far been confined within a fenced-in area, used to enjoy the long walk to the showers. On the way we could see the big, mud-brown kitchen building flanked by the clamps of beetroot (once used as cattle fodder, now our staple food source), other shacks surrounded by barbed-wire, and the broad dirt track road slicing through the center of the camp that led to the gates and the free world. Once in the showers, we would hand over our clothes for disinfection and were permitted several minutes under a single showerhead, three or four women at a time.

There was a pregnant woman in our section. When the time came for her to give birth, arrangements were made to send her to hospital in the nearby town of Celle. Although it was strictly forbidden to correspond with the outside world, even by way of the International Red Cross, this woman took the risk and smuggled a number of letters out of the camp. The Gestapo found out, and Kommandant Haas was livid with rage, claiming that we had all betrayed his trust, repaying goodness by deceit. The mother and her newborn child were dragged up front during morning roll call, and a Gestapo officer delivered her a good few kicks, screaming at her to divulge the names of those who had given her the letters to smuggle out. She remained silent, clutching her baby to her chest. Then the Gestapo officer drew his pistol. At that point the Camp Kommandant intervened, waving the officer away and ordering us all to remain in place. We stood there all day long, exhausted, but nevertheless grateful to the veteran Officer Haas who had saved a mother's life. At the end of the day, the Kommandant returned to inform us that there would be no food rations tomorrow and to deliver a severe reprimand to our physician, Dr. Grossfeld, for "criminal conspiracy."

The Spanish Compound was surrounded by barbed wire and a high wooden palisade that isolated us (the so called "privileged") from the rest of the Belsen prisoners. But even such a barrier could not shut out the cries of anguish. Night by night we could hear appeals for help screamed out in Yiddish, Polish, Russian, even English. We never heard any shooting; they had other killing systems by now. In the morning, peering through cracks in the wooden fence, we could see prisoners dragging wooden handcarts filled with corpses.

During the summer of 1944 several groups bearing foreign passports were sent out from the Spanish Compound. We never knew where they went, although they all hoped and prayed that they were being set free. Later on I learned that few of those who held certificates for Palestine ever reached the Red Cross refugee camp at Vitell in the south of France. (Journalists who visited Vitell would file reports about being impressed by the "humane treatment of the hostages.") Most of the people sent out were apparently transferred (in Red Cross cars!) to Auschwitz, never to be heard from again.

These transports steadily thinned out the hostage population. Out of 2,000, only 350 of us still remained. By now both Tommy and I were "old lags": experienced jailbirds that knew all the ropes and could give a hint here and there to the newcomers, and now and then even a word of encouragement.

Then we were moved again, this time to a dank, lice-ridden shack next to the "Dutch Compound." Conditions deteriorated; rations were cut; we began to starve. When one of our group appealed to the camp authorities, he was told (by a German clerk) that we should be thankful we were still alive.

A scribbled note slipped through the wire from the neighboring Dutch Compound read, "Exchange of about three hundred from our camp in the next few days. Transport includes a hundred of you." In the meantime we had heard nothing.

The next morning soldiers surrounded one of the shacks in the Dutch Compound, and ordered the occupants to come out and stand in line for a baggage check. They were marched off to the main gate and from there, as I heard after the war, onto a train to Vienna – and to freedom. We, the "Palestinians," were left abandoned in Bergen-Belsen.

In the autumn of 1944 Bergen-Belsen was turned into a massive transit camp. Columns of Jews from Greece, from Rumania, from Russia, and even distant Tripoli would file in. Some remained in the camp, most were marched onward.

This rush of transports through Belsen could only mean that the Germans were liquidating Jewish labor camps and ghettos. It also meant, as we gradually came to realize, that the German army was in retreat, that they were, in fact, losing the war. We could even glimpse it in the tense expressions on the faces of our German captors.

FRIDAY: about a hundred children trudge in a line, guarded by German troops. They gape at the barbed wire, at the wooden shacks. The little girls cling to their dolls, the older kids support the younger, many are weeping bitterly. That evening, I learned a few details from the kitchen crew who brought us our food:

The Germans had been employing Dutch diamond polishers, promising them that as long as they worked hard, no harm would befall their families. The diamond polishers worked as hard as they could, but nevertheless, the Germans had separated their children from their mothers and sent them here to Bergen-Belsen.

That same night I hold Tommy close, terrified that one day

they might take him away from me. He was only eight years old but seemed to sense my fear.

"Should I sing you a song, Mama?"

"Yes, Tommy, please sing to me. But quietly. People are trying to catch some sleep."

SEVENTEEN HUNDRED JEWS from Hungary are housed in the huts adjoining our compound. Lax discipline among the guards allows for a few hasty exchanges of information. The Hungarians tell of Allied victories and claim that the war will be over in a few months. We talk of Belsen and the fate of our brethren.

"A whole year and a half in a camp?!" The Hungarians seemed to be amazed.

"One year, seven months."

"They told us that we'd be in Switzerland in a matter of days!"

One of our "Palestinians" starts to say, "That's what they told us." Then he bites his tongue and falls silent.

These Hungarians were optimistic, their voices loud and hearty. It had been a long time since we had seen such energetic people. They had things we had long forgotten: fruits, hard cheese, even chocolate. They were quite generous in handing out such goodies and would watch our kids gaze at a rosy apple, rubbing it on a sleeve until it began to shine, hesitating to bite into it, and finally gnawing avidly at its juicy flesh.

We were soon eagerly bartering with them, even though we had little to offer in exchange. I mustered up the courage to suggest to one of the men on the other side of the fence that I unravel his ragged sweater and knit him a new one. He readily agreed and offered me the astronomical sum of seven cigarettes. I got to work at once. Tommy helped me by holding the skeins as I balled the wool, and the job was done within a week. Seven cigarettes could buy more than two hunks of bread.

The Germans had begun to reinforce the guards along the fence, preventing us from approaching the wire and talking with our neighbors. So we arranged that I would hang the sweater on the fence and that my customer would stuff the payment into one of the pockets. Later on, I would drift across and extract the cigarettes. Then he could take it down whenever he got the chance.

As luck would have it, the sweater was hanging on the fence when Kommandant Haas happened to pass by. I watched in terror as he ordered one of his escorts to pluck it down with his rifle. As he did so, clumsily, some of the precious cigarettes spilled from the pocket.

"Whose garment is this?" the Kommandant demanded.

My Hungarian client came forward, claiming it as his own.

"And these cigarettes?" Haas was insistent.

I approached him hesitantly, trying to explain that they, in fact, belonged to me as payment for knitting the sweater, so I could get food for my son. Haas was furious, and the Hungarian was dragged off to solitary confinement.

"And as for you, Hilde Huppert, I'll settle this account later!"

I was sure Tommy would soon be an orphan, but times were changing: Adolf Haas was soon deposed, and somehow the affair was forgotten.

Over the months, the Hungarians' hopes to leave for Switzerland began to dwindle, but one day they were ordered to prepare for a move, and once again we were ignored.

We stood by the fence, watching the convoy depart. Some of the Hungarians waved goodbye, calling out "don't despair" and "see you soon." One of these was a tall fellow whose name I never knew: he was wearing the sweater I had knitted for him.

There was a certain comfort in the knowledge that they were smuggling out a list of all the detainees in our camp. We hoped they could deliver it to the International Red Cross, which was, in fact, what happened. The Hungarians also left behind a legacy: a request to the camp Kommandant that all food parcels addressed to them be handed over to us.*

That same week, 160 Jews from Slovakia were crammed into our already overcrowded huts. Soon enough, the shacks across the fence were filled by another transport of Hungarians. These came from the labor camps and were pitiful wrecks dressed in rags. They, too, had the same sing-song accent, but they spoke in undertones.

One day on our way to the shower block, we passed a group of S.S. officers in their uniforms. They checked us with a steely glance, seemingly puzzled at the sight of prisoners walking with towels slung around their necks. My first reaction was one of fear, which swiftly turned to hatred. Some of our companions recognized officers who had taken part in the liquidation of the ghettos in Warsaw and in Cracow.

Back in our hut we soon learned that Adolf Haas had been relieved of his post and had been replaced by a certain Josef Kramer, an S.S. officer from Auschwitz. At our first encounter with Kramer, who was later to be known as the "Beast of Belsen," the new Kommandant proclaimed that we would no longer be allowed to take showers.

"You'll not be pampered by me!"

The arrival of Kramer opened a new era in the history of Bergen-Belsen, which was then to become the terminal station for tens of thousands of Jews from all corners of Europe.

The Red Army offensive forced the Germans to liquidate the labor camps in the vicinity of the battlefront. The inmates were marched on foot to Belsen, and many perished along the way. Those

---

* Many years later I saw a copy of the list that had been smuggled out by the brave Hungarians in the archives of the Jewish Agency in Jerusalem. The list, with our names on it, had been published in the Hebrew Press, and someone informed my father that Hilde and Tommy were still alive and being detained in Bergen-Belsen. The fact that our names were mentioned in the press probably saved our lives.                                    *T.S. Huppert*

who survived could be seen limping past our huts, famished, frozen, and exhausted. As they shambled past our compound, these human wraiths gazed in amazement at our children crowded along the wire, seeking their own children who had been snatched away from them. They must have found it hard to believe that there were any Jewish children left alive in Europe.

A ten-year-old girl, who had been interned here with her aunt, suddenly started to scream: "Mama! Mama!" A woman began to stumble towards our fence, only to be beaten back by the German soldier using his rifle butt. Order was swiftly restored, and the column continued on its way.

Newcomers to Belsen were housed at first in tents, and it was there that the slow death began. Hunger, typhus, disease, and beatings by the guards were swift to take their toll. The dead were cremated in a vast furnace that burned day and night; wherever you turned, you couldn't avoid the black smoke and the acrid stench of charred flesh.

The neighboring hut, which had once housed the Hungarians, was now filled with newcomers: human skeletons who could barely move or speak. They would open a gaping mouth, point at it with a bony finger, and beg for something to eat. We would gather together whatever we could, and at twilight shove a few portions of bread through the wire. The moment we slipped away, savage struggles would break out between the starving only to be silenced by warning shots from the watchtower.

NINE IN THE EVENING: Most of the people are sleeping, but I lie awake. I glance at Tommy lying by my side and can imagine him playing with Ruthy. A sudden shout awakens all.

"*Los! Los!* Get moving!"

The voices seem to be close. Then we realize they are coming from the neighboring hut where the new inmates are housed. We do our best to calm our frightened children, and huddle wide-eyed on our narrow wooden bunks. We can hear the muffled sound of blows of whips, and the cries of the victims.

"Help us, Almighty God. Hear our prayer!"

The door bursts open, and a shadowy figure stands on the threshold. He begs hoarsely for water. Someone hands him a cup from which he gulps, holding it in his bloodstained, trembling hands.

"They came and beat us up, beat us to death. I got out of there, got across the fence. Can I stay with you?"

Silence. We all know what will happen if the Germans find a fugitive in our midst, but he still was pleading: "I will hide under the bunks, no one will know. Just give me a drink of water and a slice of bread. Even half a slice."

"We've a lot of children here," says a voice out of the darkness, one of the mothers.

"Children?!"

"If they find you here they'll shoot the kids as well." Another woman's voice.

"So I can't stay?"

"No, you can't." This, a man's voice, choking back the tears.

We give him bread and water. Someone offers a precious cigarette, and as it is lit, we can see his haggard face for the first time. He takes a long drag on the smoke, coughs heavily, mumbles his thanks, and shuffles out.

THAT KIND OF SLAUGHTER went on night after night. The hut opposite us turned into a death cell. Each morning, after a night of nightmares, we could see the prisoners and the kapos flinging bodies and dismembered limbs into the courtyard. The pile would only be collected at midday when the area was "cleaned up," but the next morning there would be another mute assemblage. There was no way we could prevent the children from hearing or seeing these horrors. Tommy's already thin features grew even paler; there was no trace left of innocence or of childhood. The cremation furnace worked full blast, but still couldn't cope with the workload. In order to solve the problem, the Germans ordered the prisoners to dig mass graves into which the bodies were haphazardly flung. Bergen-Belsen, under command of master butcher Josef Kramer, became a death camp. They didn't use gas in Belsen. The victims – starved, weak, and diseased – were beaten to death.*

We were again shifted to other huts: Kommandant Kramer was expanding his area of death cells. They now included the huts where we used to live.

The transports continued flowing into Bergen-Belsen. I would stand at the fence for hours, searching for a familiar face. One day a long column of women was halted opposite our compound. Suddenly I could hear one of them calling my name. It took me a few moments to recognize Hilde Eckert, one of my fellow workers from the sweatshops in the Rzeszow Ghetto. It was a hurried, frantic conversation through the wire.

"What do you know of my family? Mama, Sigmund, Ruthy?"

"Auschwitz," she mumbled, "the gas chambers. We've just come from Auschwitz."

"All of them?"

She nodded, silently. I could find no words to reply. Looking down I could see Tommy at my side, holding my hand.

"Should I sing for you?" he asked hesitantly.

"Not now!" I screamed at him.

When I looked up, Hilde Eckert had already slipped back into line, and the column was trudging off.

So now I knew.

---

* Later, upon facing the British court martial as a war criminal, Kramer would claim that to the best of his knowledge the troops under his command had treated the prisoners in a "human fashion." His judges preferred to believe the piles of corpses and the testimonies of the survivors, and imposed the death sentence on him and nine of his compatriots. He was executed on December 12, 1945.

STARVATION REIGNED, people developed potbellies, some died of famine. One day a van with Red Cross markings pulled up next to our compound. Its doors were thrown open to reveal neat stacks of cardboard cartons. These were the food parcels sent to the Hungarians and were now being handed over to us. As we ripped the packages apart we gazed at the packets of biscuits, bags of sugar, raisins, cans of condensed milk, and processed meat as if we could hardly believe our eyes. When we got our share I began to plan a strict dietary regimen for Tommy and myself so the food would last a long, long time.

The taste of that syrupy-sweet milk still lingers. Those Red Cross food parcels saved many lives. Still, however stringent we were with ourselves, the supply didn't last all that long and hunger soon gnawed at us again. The kids would stand by the fence, waiting for the handcart that would bring the ever-thinner gruel from the kitchen, with the accompanying crusts of bread. Sometimes one of them would come rushing in, crying: "They brought the food!" and we would all run out, tin plates and cups in hand, only to discover that it wasn't the food cart, but the death wagon passing by. By now the starved and beaten prisoners no longer bothered to cover the corpses with sacks.

FEBRUARY 1945 – freezing cold outside: For some reason we were ordered to the shower block. We dragged our frozen feet through the snow and washed ourselves in icy water, while our clothes were being disinfected. On emerging from this agony, I found that my warm winter coat, which also doubled as our blanket, was missing. I was in total despair, as my only sweater had long ago been traded for bits of bread. I reported the loss to the shower orderly. He promised to look for it, but I could tell from the look in his eye that he wasn't about to make any special effort. Seeing me only in my flimsy dress, Tommy offered me his little checkered jacket.

"I've got a sweater."

"Thank you, but it's too small for me anyway."

"So tell the officer in charge."

I was persuaded, and when I spoke to the officer little Tommy also approached him in his perfect German.

"Sir, it's the only coat my Mama possesses."

"Get back into line. I'll check it out."

The following morning our hut leader and I were summoned to the camp's administrative offices. The route led past our former shacks. Dead bodies, the victims of last night's beatings, laid in the yard in rows of five. They looked like no more than skin and bones. The survivors were on parade for a head count; supporting one another, barely able to stand on their feet. Most of them were gazing dully at their late cellmates lying at their feet. Off to one side a human skeleton kneeled before a guard. The prisoner had an ear stuffed into his mouth. Our German escort explained that the man was being punished for attempting to cannibalize the corpses.

"I was also shocked when I saw that sort of thing for the first time," the soldier admitted, "but you get used to it."

At the administrative block my coat was returned to me.

I made a vow never to look again at the "Death-Cell Compound," but I couldn't keep it. As if hypnotized, I would stare at the wretched, trying to etch the faces of the victims and the eyes of their slaughterers into my memory.

Back in the hut, Tommy was delighted to see the coat. He wondered why I was looking so depressed. I told him I was tired and had a headache. That night I dreamed of corpses. Rows upon rows of dead bodies. Victims free of any guilt.

WE WENT ON LIVING. Most of the children in the hut would cry out for food, but not Tommy. His big blue eyes, progressively sinking deeper and deeper into his tiny wizened face, were the only witnesses to his hunger.

We could tell that something was going wrong. Order and

discipline weren't what they used to be. Roll calls were irregular; new edicts became rarer; it seemed as if the Germans had other problems on their minds.

There was only one barbed-wire fence between us and the kitchen compound, which lay just across Bergen-Belsen's "Main Street": a dirt track trampled hard by tens of thousands of people on their march of suffering. Over there was our food – the beetroot-clamps. Despite the risks, some of the men would venture across and scamper back with the precious cattle fodder concealed under their shirt. Others paid with their lives, and were shot down, their bodies left to rot on the food pile.

It was already the spring of 1945. We began to barter with the German guards. One evening I beckoned to an elderly soldier, pointing at my wristwatch. Clambering down from the watchtower, he approached the fence and asked, "How much?"

"Fifteen cigarettes and a loaf of bread."

"Very pricey. Ten cigarettes and a loaf," he suggested.

I agreed.

The following evening he handed over a full loaf of bread wrapped in a newspaper and a handful of cigarettes. I gave him my Swiss-made Doxa, a gift from Walter, which I had managed to keep all these years.

"Forgive me Walter," I was muttering, "but Tommy's hungry."

"What's all that?" The guard sounded agitated.

"I was counting the cigarettes."

"Don't you trust the word of a German soldier?" I had nothing to say to that. "So take the stuff and get back to your hut. I don't want the sergeant to see me." And he lumbered his way back to the watchtower with my watch.

It was only then that I realized that I had a deep scratch on my wrist from the barbed wire. Licking the wound, I raced to our hut.

"Did it work?" an anxious Tommy asked.

"Yes," I replied, hiding the loaf under our mattress.

"You're bleeding. Does it hurt?"

"No," I lied.

Only when all were asleep did Tommy and I begin to eat as quietly as possible.

"Want another bite?" I whispered. With gleaming eyes Tommy gulped down a little more, but then he gave up.

"There'll be more tomorrow," I comforted my boy.

"Hilde, I smell the bread (a voice from the neighboring bunk), give me a bit."

I did. Then a hand extended from another bunk, so I gave another bit; then more and more. No one said anything. There were only those outstretched fingers in the darkness. Feeling like a thief caught red-handed, I broke the bread into the smallest possible portions and stuffed them into the mute, demanding hands, which soon left my own empty. I could hear whispers of thanks and a blessing for the Lord's bounty. When the loaf was finished I could still feel the groping hands, the probing fingers begging for more. It was a relief to be able to declare "There's no more bread left."

Then I curled up under the meager covers near the frightened boy.

"Don't worry, Tommy. We still have the cigarettes!" I assured my little partner.

The newspaper in which the bread had been wrapped brought good tidings. The Germans were in retreat on all fronts. The retreats were defined as a "strategic withdrawal for redeployment." It was explained that, "The Fuehrer plans a major offensive that will decide the outcome of the war." But in the small print were the call-up notices for old men and young boys, and the extensive lists of those dead or missing in action. Together with the propaganda slogans aimed at bolstering public morale, this gave an even truer picture. We read this paper over and over. We read between the lines, and rejoiced.

I later learned that during this period one of the Hungarian prisoners had heard that a friend of his, a noted physician in Budapest, was incarcerated in the death cell. He then came up with a madcap scheme. By bribing one of the German guards he managed to sneak the body of a prisoner, who had starved to death, into the death cell compound, and smuggle out his friend, the doctor. The head count the following morning showed no discrepancy, there were no problems in compiling the lists. This kind of trick could only have been possible during the chaos that reigned in Bergen-Belsen during the final weeks before the liberation.

New transports informed us that the British Army was not far. There were rumors that the Germans were planning to move the hostages out, before the camp was overrun, and that we would be held as ransom for the safety of their own skin.

Bergen-Belsen was liberated by the British Army on April 15, 1945. At that time the camp held some sixty thousand inmates, most of them Jewish. The prisoners were exhausted and undernourished and sick. Many had typhus or dysentery. Some fifteen thousand died from these conditions shortly after liberation. But we were not there when the British arrived.

THE ORDER TO MOVE came on April 4. We were told to take minimal luggage and sturdy shoes (as if we had any!). The same held good for the Hungarians. We assembled for head count and were marched off to the train station, a column of semi-starved wretches trudging reluctantly toward an unknown destination.

There were about twenty cattle cars for about two thousand people. The Germans sat in their own carriage, right after the engine. The train creaked its way along the damaged tracks, which had only recently been temporarily repaired. At one point we were attacked by a high-flying American fighter plane, which fortunately missed us.

Ruined railway stations: an encouraging sight. Roads over-crowded with German refugees fleeing the Allied bombers. "Don't go that way!" they yell at us. "The Americans are near!" "That's all right with us!" we yell back, drunk with joy. Our enthusiasm was replaced by anxiety as we approached the front line. We began to fear that the Germans might kill us just before the liberation. Our fears were set at rest by the S.S. officer in charge of the transport. He went into hurried consultations with our group leaders, explaining that his orders were to bring us through Magdeburg.

"If I encounter the Allied forces, I have to activate the explosives in one of the carriages and blow up the whole train. However, I am open to a deal. You give me something of value, you put a good word for me with the Americans, and I order my troops to scram. Agreed?"

And so a diamond exchanged hands, and he was rewarded with a scribbled letter of recommendation.

The train halted by the forest, about three kilometers from Magdeburg. Some of the German soldiers bolted into the woods with the loot they had collected over the years. Some others sat down with us on the railway embankment. And we waited.

## Chapter 7
## LIBERATION

THE EARLY RAYS of a red dawn were licking at the treetops of a still-darkened forest, the birds were beginning to twitter, and we could hear the heavy gunfire in the distance getting closer.

The first American Jeep passed by at about ten in the morning, an iron bar across its front bumper searching for booby-traps and a radio mast waving madly in its rear. It was manned by four G.I.'s with steel helmets coated in dust. They pulled up and approached us warily: a motley crowd of women and children together with a couple of men here and there, all clad in rags and tatters. We must have been a pitiful sight.

"Who are you?" they demanded.

"Hello friends!" we shouted back in a chorus. "We love you! We are Jews."

They slipped off their helmets and mopped their brows, one of them pointed to the Star of David he wore on a chain around his neck.

"So am I."

The S.S. officer and what was left of his command were now coming forward to lay down their weapons. Executing a perfect parade ground salute, the officer formally declared the surrender of his forces. After glancing at him, and then at us, the American sergeant drew his pistol.

One of our group hastily intervened.

"We promised this man his life in return for ours. He saved us."

"Too bad," replied the American.

He then ordered the S.S. officer and his men to wait at the side of the road. We were all trying to talk to the Jewish G.I. but he knew very little Yiddish, and our English was totally inadequate. We asked him about his relatives, desperate to find some family link with this Jewish fighter who carried a gun.

The reconnaissance Jeep (that was all it was) had to go on its way, but before it did, the G.I. called up his battalion headquarters and reported finding a large group of Jewish survivors.

"Don't worry," one of our men was saying, "we'll watch over the Nazis."

It took some hours before more Americans arrived with crates of bread and canned food. An improvised field-kitchen was set up along the roadside and a cheery cook began preparing a hot meal. The G.I.'s were warm and friendly, eager to listen, but seemingly unable to believe what they were hearing. They were trying to be helpful; and as for us, we were hugging and kissing all of them out of sheer relief and gratitude.

I was questioned by a young officer about who I was and where I came from. I did my best in my basic English to tell him about Bergen-Belsen, a place he had never heard of. He kept asking me why my family should have been slaughtered, whether I had any concrete proof, was I certain the Germans had gas chambers.

I invited others to tell him about what the Germans had done to them and their families: he was doing his best to comprehend a hitherto unknown reality, repeating all the time in an undertone, "That's just impossible."

When we eventually parted, he asked me if there was anything he could do for me. There was: "Try and make contact with my cousin, George Pillersdorf in Cleveland, Ohio. Here's his address. Tell him that Hilde and Tommy are alive. He'll be able to notify my husband in Palestine."

The young officer promised to do so, and kept his word. Only a few days after we won our freedom, Walter found out we had survived.

Many of our group were escorted by the Americans to the nearby German village of Fahlsleben. Others, including Tommy and myself, waited for ambulances to take us to the town of Hillersleben. Just as I was getting on board, I suddenly saw a little blonde girl around Tommy's age seated on her bundle. I recognized her as an orphan called Lily whose father had been shot in the Warsaw Ghetto and whose mother had starved to death at Bergen-Belsen. In the camp she had been cared for by her mother's friends; here she was all alone. She sat there watching the people boarding the vehicles, weary and indifferent to all that was going on around her.

"Lily," I called, "Why don't you get on board."

"Me? I've got no one to go with."

"So come with us. Give Tommy your hand."

Tommy was hesitant for a moment, but then extended a welcome. Lily slowly rose to her feet.

"I don't need your hand. I'll come, but I'll come alone."

"So get a move on!"

"I'm coming."

And so, reluctantly, Lily joined us.

In Hillersleben the Americans housed us in the apartments of German civilians, who were ordered to evacuate. Tommy, Lily, and I were sent to an elegant villa where a German woman met us at the gate demanding to know what we wanted. After I explained to her that we had been sent by the Americans, she begrudgingly led us to the top floor, doing her best to prevent us from catching a glimpse of the richly-furnished living room.

"Where are you from?" she asked Tommy.

"From Bergen-Belsen, do you know what that is?"

"*Nein.*"

"It's a concentration camp where the Germans killed Jews."

"Why do you spread such lies, boy?" she protested.

"It's the truth," Tommy insisted. "I was there. The Germans killed my Grandma, and my Grandpa, and Ruthy. Ruthy was my best friend."

"Tell me, madam," the woman was appealing to me now, "was it really all that bad?"

"Ask your father, ask your husband, ask your brothers."

"I can't believe it," she muttered to herself.

"So where did you get two pianos, antique oil-paintings, precious porcelain, and so many Persian carpets? Did you have all that before the war?"

"My husband sent them." She was both blushing and stammering. "We had conquered cities, we were victors."

Before leaving she approached me as if to say goodbye: "I was always opposed to the Nazi regime."

Getting cold comfort from me, she hurriedly slunk away dragging two suitcases that were probably over-stuffed with valuables. I ushered the children into a gleaming clean bedroom:

"Before you go to bed you've both got to take a bath."

They stared at the beds, at the pillows, and the woolen blankets.

"Can't we just sit here for a moment?" Tommy pleaded.

"All right, just for a moment, then it's bath time. First Lily, then you."

I scrubbed them both down and shampooed their hair; they enjoyed the bath so much that they were begging me to let them stay submerged in the hot water. When I finally got them back to the bedroom, they leapt eagerly into bed to sleep between soft white sheets.

A portion of semolina with a few scraps of chocolate was gulped down eagerly and Tommy, encouraged by Lily, was immediately asking for a second helping. When I refused, he protested: "There's so much food here, Mama, why ration it now?"

I tried to convince him that he had to get used to eating normally stage by stage, that too much, too soon, might be bad for him. He was reluctant to accept my explanation, but didn't ask for more.

The following morning I spent quite some time with Lily. I had given her some clean undergarments and a new dress. She rushed at once to show herself off to Tommy, who said she looked nice. I could tell that he was jealous. While we had been imprisoned, his mother had been all his own. Now he was being asked to share her with some strange little girl. On the other hand, Lily was jealous of Tommy. I once heard her complaining to him, convinced that I was out of earshot, "You've got a Mama and Papa."

As former inmates of Bergen-Belsen we had no qualms about opening cabinets and drawers in a house like that. Among the papers I discovered a letter of gratitude addressed to the owner from S.S. headquarters regarding certain "successful" operations. The letter gave no particulars. There was also a letter from the owner of this palace that was sent to his fiancée on the eve of the war in which he pleaded that financial difficulties were forcing him to delay their wedding date.

From the attic to the cellars the house was stuffed with well-chosen merchandise: dozens of men's shoes in all sizes, suits, leather coats, scores of crystal vases, sets of silverware, boxes full of medicine. The owners had chosen only the best, with excellent taste and a keen nose for business.

When we invited some of our former camp inmates over to taste of the spoils, they came as fast as they could and stood there agape. U.S. Army fatigues were soon exchanged for more stylish apparel, but the expensive suits and elegant dresses hung on their

gaunt bodies like costumes handed down from one theatrical performance to another. Here and there I noticed that some of them
were wearing more than one suit or more than one dress.

After a few days of rest and recuperation I went to the American headquarters and asked for a job. Since I spoke some English
and was fluent in German I was placed in the liaison bureau that
dealt with the local German population. Listening daily to the
appeals of the citizens, it appeared that most of these people, who
were famous for their *"Ordnung und Diszipline,"* had happened to
have misplaced their identity papers and were now applying for
new ones. They were all anxious to erase their past, trying to forget
it – or have it be forgotten.

The Germans were cringing before the American victors, overdoing their polite manners and appreciation. All traces of Aryan
pride had been shattered with the collapse of the Thousand Year
Reich. Poison pen letters reached us every day, neighbor denounc-
ing neighbor:

"So-and-so now applying for employment with the U.S. authorities was a Nazi Party activist between the years such-and-such."

Totally sickened by this, the Americans would send any in-
former who appeared in their office packing, along with a severe
reprimand and a can of corned beef.

Hordes of Germans protested that they had never supported
Hitler, others stressed that they had never heard of the camps. They
all claimed that the atrocities were carried out by fringe groups and
that the German people had been totally unaware.

Despite the devoted care of the Americans, many of the camp
survivors perished in the hospitals. They were too weak and too
broken. Help had come too late.

Those who actually recovered began to seek ways to go home.
The Americans organized convoys to transport Jews to France,
Belgium, and Holland. Jews from Eastern Europe faced a different
dilemma. They had no wish to return to those countries in which

their relatives had been slaughtered, there was nothing left for them there.

Many of us appealed to the American authorities to let them go to Palestine, but the reply was deeply disappointing. The American officer in charge devoted quite some time to explaining the situation. Only those holding Palestinian certificates would be allowed in. To all others, the gates of the Promised Land were locked. We raised our voices in protest, screaming that this was a travesty of justice. The officer seemed to agree with us.

DESPITE THE AGONY of European Jewry, despite the fact that a Jewish Brigade from Palestine was fighting with the Allied Forces in Europe, the British Government was still imposing an embargo on Jewish refugees striving to reach their ancient homeland.

Our group included many orphans whose parents had been murdered by the Nazis. Their adoptive parents, who had kept them alive during the war, were now penniless. They were trying their best to build a new life and could no longer shoulder the burden of the adopted children. They wanted to hand them over to someone they could trust.

One day we were visited by an American military chaplain, a young rabbi who had already heard about the camps and was looking for ways to help the survivors. I told him about the orphans and he promised to get in touch with the Joint Distribution Committee in Paris.

"You, Mrs. Huppert, will be going with the first group. I'm sure your husband will be happy to see you both."

The rabbi was as good as his word. Within two weeks we had a visit from a nurse by the name of Miss Neufeld. She had been sent by the Red Cross and the JDC to organize a group of orphans from Bergen-Belsen and Buchenwald to be sent to Palestine via France. We quickly became close friends. She was an energetic and efficient young woman who was readily able to understand what we had been through. Miss Neufeld raised no objection when she saw I had included some slightly older people (age twenty or more) on the list of applicants:

"They're orphans too, you know," I apologized.

"Don't worry about that! You just take care of the kids and I'll take care of permits and transportation."

I started making the rounds of the local hospitals collecting orphans and children whose fathers were in Palestine. Their mothers would just have to await their turn. Some of the kids refused point-blank to go alone: "Sure I want to go, sure I want to see my father, but I'm not leaving my mother here by herself," they would say.

"We've been hostages for years!" one of the women cried angrily. "Why should I have to wait now?"

I, the lucky one, had no answer for her.

I took my leave from the American commander, thanking him for all his kindness and understanding. As he shook my hand he said, "If I hadn't seen you all for myself, I'd never have been able to believe all those stories."

I returned his salute with a heartfelt kiss on his cheek.

Our five heavy-duty U.S. Army trucks passed first of all through Magdeburg where the orphaned children were openly delighted at the sight of the ruined, half abandoned city. Toward evening we reached Weimar (Goethe's city from another civilization), and then Buchenwald, whose grim watchtowers dominated the skyline from afar. We drove through the gates of this infamous concentration camp in something resembling a victory parade. The children sang; the newly-freed inmates were thronging what had once been the site of the daily head count, gazing in wonder at the Jewish children who had survived. Many, I suspect, were searching in vain for their own children. Here we collected a group of youngsters, all of them eager to reach Palestine.

In Buchenwald we were housed in what had formerly been the residence of the S.S. officers and were served an excellent meal by the camp quartermaster, a German communist incarcerated here throughout the war. The children were beginning to fill out, look healthier, and walk about more confidently. They no longer spoke in hushed voices.

As for me, I felt that I still hadn't tasted real freedom. I was still in a camp surrounded by barbed wire. True, the gates were open and the authorities were our allies, but it was a long way from my husband and my home.

In charge of our group (from the moment we arrived at Buchenwald) was Rabbi Dr. Abraham Marcus. At our first meeting I told him as much as I knew about the personal histories of all the young people I had brought with me. As I did so, I recalled the girl who had seen her mother when that last transport had arrived at Bergen-Belsen.

"Maybe she is still alive," I pondered aloud. "We have the girl with us. She never stops talking about her mother."

"We'll see if something can be done," Rabbi Marcus responded.

The following day the rabbi drove off in a Jeep, taking the little girl back to Bergen-Belsen and returning later aglow with satisfaction. Mother and child were reunited.

We brought ninety-six children from Bergen-Belsen; by the time we added the "older children" from Buchenwald, our ranks had swollen to 530. I divided the children into groups and appointed ten of the older boys and girls as guardians over the little ones. They worked with a will and it was a joy to watch the teamwork. Tommy and Lily were officially part of one of the "younger" groups, but they still slept with me in my hut.

One of the ex-inmates of Buchenwald took me on a guided tour of the vast Men's Compound. Up to a few weeks before the liberation this camp had housed some seventy thousand prisoners, who had been assigned to forced labor at local factories. My companion described the conditions and the so-called "medical experiments." He mentioned that German protestors against the Nazi rule had also been sent here. Those inmates, he told me, had helped out as best they could, often hiding Jewish children in their barracks.

Our last stop was the gigantic crematorium crowded with G.I.'s taking snapshots. I had thought I was immune to anything by now, but staring into the gaping jaws of those ovens still partly filled with the half-charred bones of human beings, I knew I was mistaken.

"Take me out of here," I begged my guide. "But fast!"

By six the following morning we were at the Buchenwald railway station. Many from the camp had come to cheer us on our way, and the carriages in which we were destined to roll across Germany were decorated with huge placards: "We are orphans from Bergen-Belsen and Buchenwald"; "Murderers, where are our parents?"

WE WERE IN HIGH SPIRITS throughout the journey as we watched the landscape pass by: the ruined German cities, the long bridge across the Rhine, the Ardennes peaks, and finally the picturesque villages of France. At the border we were greeted by officials of the International Red Cross and transferred into cozy Pullman cars. Everyone was very considerate and treated us as gently as possible, like invalids. It was nice to be pampered, to enjoy the avuncular attitude of Rabbi Marcus, but there was something that gnawed at me deep down. One began to resent their concern. It was as if our benefactors were trying to atone for something, to salve their own consciences.

In Paris we were welcomed by representatives of the Jewish community, which was still struggling to reorganize itself. Housed in the luxurious Hotel Luticea, we were often visited by French Jewish families searching for their children taken from them by the Germans. Whenever they came there was a glimmer of hope in their eyes, and whenever they left, I could see them patting our little orphans on the head, then turning irresolutely away, the husband clutching the wife's hand, the wife supporting her husband.

We were shown the sights of Paris for a whole week: Versailles, the Zoological Gardens, and the Eiffel Tower. One night a few youngsters slipped out to a night club. Rabbi Marcus had a word with me and said that they should get a good reprimand. I couldn't agree: they had only been fulfilling some of the deepest desires we had all longed for, for so long – to taste the sweet, heady flavor of freedom.

Afterwards I was assigned to take all the younger children on vacation to the Chateau de Boisse la Bertram just outside Paris. This lasted for some weeks during which the kids ran scampering through the woods, swam in the Seine, and watched the boats going through the locks; I could hear their laughter all day long. But at night I could hear their screams as they woke up from nightmares.

EVENTUALLY IT BECAME CLEAR that there had been some kind of misunderstanding: the French Government seemed to think that the children were supposed to remain in France, and there were plenty of French Jews willing to adopt them. They visited the chateau almost every day, bearing gifts and tempting offers. One of the dignitaries of the Jewish community even suggested that I take Tommy and Lily with me to Palestine at once, leaving the rest of the children in their care. Naturally, I refused. I saw it as my task to bring all the children to Palestine.

I appealed to Dr. Marcus, who brought in the JDC on our side. One of France's leading Christian clergyman also intervened, and eventually the permits were granted. At our farewell celebration, the chief rabbi of France, Yehuda Nadish, delivered a moving speech and we all sang Hatikvah – the anthem of hope.

FOR MOST OF US a sea voyage was an exhilarating experience. We would stroll along the deck breathing in the salty air, watching the seagulls, and seeking a sign of land on the horizon.

Every evening we would gather in the dining hall to sing

together in Yiddish. Some of the boys and girls taught us Hebrew songs. We learned the unfamiliar words by heart and would sing them with the feeling they deserved. It was like singing a prayer, a declaration of love.

JULY 16, 1945: The first sight of Mount Carmel towered above with the white houses of Haifa descending down the slopes to welcome us. As we docked at the Haifa port there were Jewish Agency officials and armed British soldiers awaiting us on the pier. No relatives were allowed within the port area. It was a disturbing reception. It became even more ominous when we were loaded onto army trucks and driven off to a transit camp known as Athlith. Again barbed wire and watchtowers.

All we wanted was to get away.

At Athlith we were subjected to medical examinations and sprayed with D.D.T. disinfectant. The British soldiers treated us quite properly, but we could not help comparing them with other soldiers we had known.

It was in Athlith that I caught my first glimpse of my husband, Walter, and my brother David. They had been waiting for hours outside the Haifa port, but hadn't been allowed inside. Now they were there, on the other side of the barbed wire. I pointed them out to Tommy:

"The tall man, over there, waving to us, that's Papa!"

"He looks nice. Do you think he's got a car?"

I was laughing, hoisting Tommy high. Father and son waved to each other.

When they let us out after three days, Walter took us in a taxi to his one-room apartment, half way up Haifa's Mount Carmel. On the way he explained to me that he now ran a small leather goods shop with a woman who could easily be replaced just as soon as I felt up to getting back to work.

"After all, you're an experienced saleswoman."

It seemed to me a bit early to be discussing all this. I was also wondering what role this unknown woman was playing in Walter's life. I later learned that Mania (that was her name) was a decent woman and there was nothing between her and my loyal husband.

MOST OF THE CHILDREN I HAD BROUGHT with me were placed in boarding schools run by the Youth Immigration movement known as Aliyat Hanoar, headed by Henrietta Szold. Some were adopted by kibbutzim (collective settlements), others found a home with surviving relatives.

Lily represented something of a problem. I could see that she and Tommy did not get along. It was Henrietta's Szold's deputy, Hans Beyth, who persuaded me that I must rebuild a new life with a husband I hadn't seen for so many years, and that a one-room apartment was no place to tackle the problems of a foster daughter. He found a home for Lily in a kibbutz in the Jerusalem hills.

*THE DAYS AND YEARS HAVE PASSED BY. The children have grown, but they still come to visit me. Some send postcards from faraway places. We have a common suffering that binds us together.*

*I live in the ancient homeland of the Jewish people, where my second son, Shlomo, was born a sabra. We are happy and content here in spite of the dangers, in spite of the wars. This is my home.*

*But I shall never forget.*

# A Toast for Bertha
## A Short Novel

## by Son: *SHMUEL THOMAS HUPPERT*

Despite the fact that the author did revisit his hometown in 1990, this is a work of fiction. True, the names of his family members are authentic, but everything else in the small Czech town, known here as T., is a mixture of vague memory and vivid imagination.

An ancient Hebrew poet, Moshe Ben Ezra, once wrote:
*"The best of a poem*
*Lies in duplicity."*

*Tommy and girl friend (Bertha?), June 1938*

THE FIRST TO GIVE IN to hunger was the slim fellow seated next to the window. Snapping his book shut, he smoothed his light-green suit, that had seen quite a few summers, and drew a thermos and brown paper bag out of his leather suitcase. Immediately, as if the bell had rung for the morning break, the elderly woman, possibly a grandmother on her way to visit her grandchildren, laid aside her knitting and produced an embroidered serviette and a parcel of food from her straw basket.

The last to succumb was the young couple, both clad in jeans with suspenders over their T-shirts, the red-headed youth sporting a single earring, who had clung to each other throughout the journey exchanging whispers, giggles, and moist kisses. The slim fellow, who looked like either a lawyer or a school inspector, flashed them a disapproving glance now and then, while the grandmother seemed to look kindly on the young lovers, chewing on her lower lip like a teenager waiting for an invitation to dance.

Our fellow travelers unwrapped their sandwiches and bit ravenously into the black bread. They sipped their coffee, and their meal filled the train compartment with steam and the pungent odor of salami and garlic. Only my wife and I failed to join in the feasting. I had already seen all four of them exchange glances and smile uneasily at us, uncertain as to whether to enter a conversation with strangers. Vaclav Havel's Velvet Revolution had freed Czechoslovakia from forty years of Soviet oppression but its citizens still felt the butterflies in their stomachs.

"Would you like an apple?" the young fellow asked me, making the offer only after consulting his rosy-cheeked girlfriend.

Summoning up all my vocabulary from childhood, I managed to stammer out an answer in a mixture of Czech and Polish, "No, thank you. Thank you very much."

I immediately began to scold myself: First of all, my mouth is watering for something to eat, and second, I'd forfeited the chance of making conversation.

The train sped by farms and villages. I saw the blackened chimneys atop the tiled roofs and wind vanes twisting in the summer breeze. Apron-clad peasants hung out their laundry; a girl in a flowered blouse scattered seed for a flock of hens reigned by a strutting rooster; I spied an old woman dragging a stubborn cow along on a rope. Sunburned children ran alongside the railroad track in a futile contest with the train. They fell flat on the dusty road; one of them bared his bottom in defiance. A solitary tractor stood idle in the corner of the field. There were cowsheds, barns, log piles, and ploughed fields as far as the eye could see; apple orchards, groves of broad-leafed maples, rustling pine trees, streams and rivers (a cause for envy for Jerusalemites coming from a barren country), villages, the town hall, the church, the marketplace, the fountain, cobblestone streets, houses faced with yellowing plaster, men strolling and smoking their clay pipes, women clustering around a street vendor, a factory built of ugly black bricks, and train stations whose upper beams, beneath their glass canopies, boasted clocks dating back to the days of Franz Joseph, the emperor who favored Jews.

Had I ever seen these sights before? When I was two or three years old Grandpa Sigmund took me on a trip from T. to the zoo in Prague on this same railroad. Perhaps we traveled in this very carriage, only now the velvet upholstery had been replaced with something cheaper, and the grandson had become a grandfather. Would such sights awaken memories that had lain dormant for almost three score years and already become fixed in a deadly slumber of forgetfulness?

AFTER EACH STOP at a major station, the conductor poked his head into the compartment (the slim sourpuss and the loving couple had gotten off by now). The conductor, over forty years old, wore glasses, had a broad forehead, and wore his cap defiantly tilted at an angle, while his faded blue uniform strained across his lax and fattening figure. Feeling hungry, I asked him, in German, to show me the way to the dining car. He shrugged his shoulders and replied, in a fairly passable German: "Management decided to get rid of it. In any case, few people have any spare cash these days, and there are fast-food counters at most of the main stopovers. And apart from that," he lowered his voice surreptitiously, glancing across at Grandma still compulsively engaged in her knitting, "it seems that the comrade who once ran the dining car worked hand-in-hand with the waitress and that together they would steal coffee and sugar to sell on the black market. There was an investigation and it was decided that..."

At this point the old woman raised her head, flashing an alarmed glance at the conductor. She laid her knitting back in her basket, crossed herself, pulled a tattered suitcase from the luggage rack, and hastened out of the compartment. The conductor, turning pale, hurried after her.

After a stopover in O., the conductor knocked on our door and asked with a shy smile whether he could have a word with us. I invited him in, and his burly body slumped gratefully onto the upholstered seat.

"From where would the lady and the gentleman be coming?" he inquired politely.

"From Israel," we told him. To our surprise, we discovered that he was well-versed in the map of the Middle East as well as the Israeli-Palestinian conflict. I shuddered at the sudden thought that he might once have been employed by the Secret Service. This was, after all, an international express train, and our guest, who seemed to know a number of languages, could have easily been going up and down the corridors eavesdropping on the conversations of innocent passengers and reporting their secrets.

"And where might you be headed, if I may ask?" he contin-ued.

"To T."

"To T. of all places?"

"Why not?" asked my wife.

"True, true. Why not?" After recovering his composure and ignoring our embarrassment, he made a swift change of subject:

"My hobby is Oriental history. When I get home after my shift, I take a bath, change my clothes, reheat some of Sunday's cabbage soup, and then I sit and read classics such as *The Codes of Hammurabi* and *The Tales of Gilgamesh*. I've studied sketches of the pyramids that your ancestors built in Egypt. I'm a great admirer of Moses, the father of all prophets. He reminds me of our President Thomas Garrigue Masaryk."

The conductor wiped a hand over his pale forehead. Then he glanced at his watch and went on in a hurried tone: "I'm fascinated in particular by the Phoenician traders, both inventors of glass and daring mariners. I even read somewhere that they were ahead of Columbus! Now and then, as I stumble my way from car to car, I imagine myself on the deck of a Phoenician galley on its way to Tyre or Carthage. I have a modest library of books about history and archeology, which I bought in second-hand bookstores. It's my dream to visit Lebanon and Egypt and Israel. Once you had to have a letter of recommendation from your place of work, a military permit, an approval from the party, a certification from the police of a clean record, and a copy of your bank account, just to get an exit visa to travel abroad. Nowadays, when you can fly off to wherever you want, it's only the rich folks who can afford it. As for me, I do my best to save a few hundred crowns a month, but last year Mother broke a hip, so I had to give something to the doctor in order to jump the line for an operation. That fracture cost me a quarter of all my savings. Apart from that, the authorities hinted that if I wanted to advance in my career, maybe get to be station-master somewhere or other, it would be better not to be stuffing my head with hieroglyphics. You should please excuse me for rambling on like this. It's been weeks since I talked with anyone."

"Don't you have any friends?" my wife asked.

"We don't trust our neighbors. If you have a friend, you take him home for a glass of Slivovitz, turn on the TV so that no one will hear anything, then you talk quietly."

"But today it's a new, free Czechoslovakia," I tried to remind him.

"I had my illusions during the Prague Spring. I had the feeling we were at last spreading our wings. Then the Russian tanks came in to run over the students and turn Dubcek into a street sweeper."

"The Soviet Union's falling apart. They won't come back to Czechoslovakia."

"That's true, sir. But for me, freedom came too late."

Afterwards we talked about Jerusalem. I took out a postcard of pilgrims on the Via Dolorosa and showed it to him; his eyes gleamed.

"It's yours," I said handing the postcard to him.

"Many thanks. I'll keep it on the mantel next to the picture of my late father."

"You were asking about food on the train. At the next station there's a kiosk run by a woman I know. I'll get off with you and buy you something to eat and drink. She'll serve me without standing in line."

"That's very kind of you."

Thanks to the conductor we soon had a couple of bottles of lemonade and two rolls stuffed with salami that a young woman with dyed blond hair, raw red hands, and an urchin grin, held out to the conductor over the heads of a complaining line of people.

"Take these to your wife," he told me. "I have to deal with the newly boarded passengers."

Back in our compartment I found a young man seated opposite my wife, long faced and blue eyed with a whiff of cologne about him. He was wearing a fashionable checkered sports jacket and a flowered silk tie; on his knees was a James Bond briefcase with a combination lock. A sharp, successful businessman, harbinger of a brave new world.

"You will mind if I smoke?" he asked in hesitant English.

"Yes," replied my wife sneezing.

"So..." he grinned, "I'll poison myself in the corridor."

We took a few gulps of the sickly yellow lemonade, that tasted mostly of saccharine, and chewed on the mustard-laden rolls. My wife, suspecting that the salami was probably made from pork, wrapped the slices in paper and stuffed them deep into the trash so that the conductor wouldn't be offended. He was back with us within a few moments. As he clipped the ticket of our new stylish companion, he seemed a little disappointed that we were no longer alone.

"Your change, sir," he said formally, handing me a few coins. Then he swiftly left the compartment, never to return. We wondered whether he would say goodbye when we reached our destination, but when we got off the train, we could see his cap bobbing up and down at the far end of the platform like a little fishing boat on the horizon.

"He's got something against this place," my wife said.

I didn't reply. I was enviously watching the people hugging long-lost relatives and friends, hoping that someone might run up to embrace me.

ALTHOUGH I KNEW THAT the family home in T. was still standing, it was obvious we would stay in a hotel. My parents, who were very excited at the idea of our trip, had weighed us down with good advice, and had given us the address of a Czech acquaintance, a certain Frau Schtiasna.

"The only decent hotel in T. used to be called Krantz," my father had told me, "after that family of Austrian aristocrats with a castle in the mountains. But after the Munich Agreement of 1938, when the town was annexed by the Poles, the landlord gave it a Polish name. I have no idea what it might have been called during the German occupation and later under communist rule. In T., flags, national anthems, and names had changed often with remarkable ease.

"I remember a restaurant on the ground floor with a small orchestra and excellent cuisine," he added. "When Papa Sigmund, your grandfather, wanted to give Mama a treat, he would say, 'Valli, put on a hat with a feather. We're eating at the hotel!'

"'A waste of good money. Mascha has made knedelichki just the way you like it.'

"'I said we're eating out!' Grandpa Sigmund knew how to be stubborn. 'I'll eat the knedelichki later.'"

Standing now on the dreary platform, I could recall my father's tales and anecdotes. My clever mother, who was born into a devout Jewish family in the Polish provinces, would listen, as if she hadn't heard that one, but never intervened.

I wanted to ask someone for directions to the hotel, but anyone I asked seemed to speak only Czech. When it became clear that I didn't speak the language, the locals reacted with a shrug of the shoulders, an endearing smile, and a sudden vanish from the scene. So we gathered our hand luggage together and descended into a dark, rather eerie exit tunnel from the station in which we turned to the right.

Out on the street I could see a square in the distance where an ancient bus was parked. I suggested that my wife take a rest while I took a look around. I then set off toward the small square, whistling a little march and wondering, just a bit, why there was no welcoming committee for the return of the prodigal son. The mayor tended to forget things, and in any case, the Fire Brigade band had a previous engagement, I told myself. I took these facts into consideration, but was not entirely comforted.

I managed to recall a few Czech words and asked the people in the square where I might find a taxi. They stared at me in amazement. A mother pushing a carriage with enormous wheels was brave enough to suggest that I try the tavern on the corner, maybe they would know there.

"The Fox and Chicken": a faded sign depicting this classic act of violence hung over the low doorway. As I opened the heavy wooden door, I was stunned by the stench within. It took a few moments to recover and for my eyes to adjust to the gloomy room lit only by small candles hanging from the low ceiling. My entry aroused little response from the men and the women seated at the tables, people talking in hoarse whispers, smoking, and staring at their empty beer glasses. On my way to the bar, I was accosted by a woman of about my age with a smile that must once have been seductive.

"Buy me a drink, mister?"

"Bertha, if you don't leave the customers alone you'll be out on your ear!" said the barrel-bellied bartender. They spoke in Czech, but I could get the gist of it.

The woman lowered her head as she licked her parched lips and mumbled, "Just a little one, mister?"

The bartender wiped the foam from a stein of beer before saying, quite gently, "Go home Bertha, you've had enough for one day.

Your man'll be home soon from the factory, and if you don't have his dinner ready he'll be mad at you."

At this point I managed to pose my question.

"Taxi?" The bartender was drumming his fingers on the bar. "Vanek used to have a 1964 Skoda, but he left here five years ago. We haven't had a taxi in T. ever since. Doesn't pay. This is a small town, who can afford such luxuries?"

"Where can I find a hotel then?" I asked in a hesitant mixture of Czech and Polish.

"Next to the station."

"Turn right in the tunnel?"

"Turn left. We're a socialist republic, or we used to be. Where would the gentleman be from?"

"From Jerusalem."

"Jesus, Maria!" He crossed himself. The drunkards were all silent now, staring at me as if I were an angel hiding its wings beneath a blue raincoat.

"And what in heaven's name would he be doing in God-forsaken T.?"

I was tempted to tell him that I was born here, but on second thought, a crowd of somnolent drunks in a stinking tavern didn't seem the best of settings for my revelation.

"I'm on a trip."

"A tourist in T.? So President Havel really did make a revolution in Prague, like they say, like we saw on television. This calls for a drink! On the house, mister, you name it."

"Drinks for everyone, it's on me. And a small schnapps for Madame Bertha."

"If you say so, sir."

The drunken woman wept openly.

"Madame Bertha! Did you hear that?"

I slapped three hundred-crown notes on the bar.

"Many thanks, sir."

The drunkards gazed in wonder at their full glasses, muttering a silent prayer. Suddenly, an elderly man wearing a relatively neat old-fashioned suit and tie got on his feet, gripped the corners of the table, and apologetically posed a question:

"Might I inquire as to the name of our honored guest so that we may raise our glasses to his health?"

"Thomas," I replied, using my original Czech name.

"Praise be to you, Mr. Thomas!" the elderly man said as he raised his glass, drank deeply, belched, and set back, deflated.

GATHERING OUR BELONGINGS, we returned to the station tunnel, its darkness seeming brighter now, familiar, almost welcoming. We took the left-hand turn and emerged into the light of day before a yellow stone building with a terrace and windows through which one could make out a ballroom of sorts. Above the broad entryway, next to the scarred and faded symbol of aristocracy, was the name of the hotel: Krantz. We tried the door. It was locked. We looked around for someone who might be able to tell us whether the hotel was in use, but saw only a small boy playing with an iron hoop. As he stared at us, the hoop finished its spin with an ear-splitting clatter. Snatching up his toy, the child was off and away, running towards the river.

From a second-story window a bald man beckoned to us, suggesting that we try the side entrance that led to the dining room. We followed his advice and found ourselves tripping over upended tables and chairs, stumbling into the corner of the bandstand, and wondering what this bald character had had in mind by beckoning us into the depths of an abandoned hotel. From the dining room we made our way into the corridor where, much to our surprise, we found an elevator. Pasted onto its door was a small sign whose significance became clear once the button was pressed. The elevator let out a muffled hum and appeared to be stuck somewhere between floors. With no other choice, we started to ascend the spiral staircase, with its threadbare crimson carpet, up to Floor 2. There, seated behind the reception desk, was the clerk who had called to us: black jacketed, white tied, clean shaven, but undeniably bottle-nosed. I greeted him in German and asked if he might have a room to spare.

After studying his registry, as if in doubt or possibly waiting for a tip, he hemmed and hawed for a moment before rising and pronouncing in perfect German: "We have a few spare rooms, almost the entire hotel in fact, apart from Room 37. This is reserved for a regular guest, the lawyer from A. He prefers this room since it is far from the dining room, where the dance band tends to raise the roof twice weekly, and also from the railroad tracks with the late-night trains that do not usually stop here, but whose drowsing drivers sound their sirens, awakening those whose windows overlook the railroad."

Taking a deep breath, he added, almost lyrically, "You'll find our T. to be a quiet town. The youngsters call it dead and run away from us to other towns where the authorities built factories, working-class neighborhoods, and supermarkets. They even shifted the regional administration. But you two must be tired from traveling. I'll open up a few rooms. Let the lady choose. By the way, you haven't told me where you come from?"

"From Israel," said my wife.

"Ah," he said as if he had known all along. "The room is for one night?"

"For three."

"For three nights in T.? Well, why not? They say that before the war – I'm new here, only thirty years – they had vacationers who'd spend a whole week, sometimes even more, here in T., hiking on the hillsides, feasting on venison in the taverns, shopping on Main Street (they renamed it Revolution Street), downing their Pilsen, and waltzing till dawn. That was before the Germans came with their flags and drums and swastikas. The Czechs never forgot the warm welcome the locals gave them. Most of the people here used to be of German origin. After the liberation this town got its just desserts.

"But you must be wanting a shower and a rest. Hot water's only at seven…Three nights? You must be on important business. I'm not nosy. They tell me there used to be a few rich Jewish families here in T., most of them in the Polish quarter. There are no Jews here today."

I took out a carton of American cigarettes I had bought on the plane and offered him a pack. It was in his pocket in a moment, even though he protested that I shouldn't have troubled.

"How much is the room?"

He produced an abacus and flicked the colored beads back and forth, making hasty notes on a scrap of gray recycled paper.

"Maybe you would like to pay in dollars? I'd be happy to exchange them. You'll get more from me than you will at the bank."

"That suits me. I'll pay you now."

The receptionist took the dollars and wrote out the receipt as if I had paid in Czech crowns. Then he asked if we needed anything else.

"Where can we get dinner in town?"

"That's a bit of a problem. The hotel dining room's closed tonight, and there's no other restaurant here in T. There are pubs, of course, where you can get a bowl of soup and a sausage, but I wouldn't recommend them. All these unemployed youngsters have been getting vicious lately, getting drunk, sniffing drugs, chasing the girls – troublemakers. And the cops, all five of them, don't want to know. There was a time when we had law and order. You'd be better off buying a few things at Pavel's grocery store. He's got dairy products, sausages, drinks, all imports. Anyone can show you the way to Pavel's place."

"What do you do here in the evening?"

"Do in the evening? Not much, sir. We don't have a concert hall or a theater. There's a movie theater next to the marketplace that's open three times a week, but not tonight. Best to come back here to the hotel and watch television. We get Austrian and German channels. We're green with envy seeing how they live over there. Now please fill in the forms and I'll show you to your room."

Grabbing a bunch of keys, he heaved himself from his cushioned chair and with an elegant gesture, invited my wife to accompany him. I was left struggling with the form, trying to decipher the Czech and managing only to register my name, passport number, and nationality before my wife came back.

"I've chosen Room 36 next to the lawyer. It's a nice room and the bathroom's quite clean. I'll just wash up and then we'll go to – "

"Yes," I interrupted. We didn't mention the word: "home."

"Can you help me fill in the form?" I asked the clerk.

"But of course, sir."

I assumed that my family name would betray me, but the clerk never batted an eyelid. He simply scribbled down the details with an experienced hand, humming a jingle in German: "From the cradle to the grave, filling forms is how we slave."

I was almost ready to tell him that I had been born in T., but in the end I said nothing. This so-called "newcomer" had only come here twenty years after my family had run away, leaving behind a house and home, our furniture, Persian carpets, treasured pictures, the vast toy train-set that Grandpa brought from Vienna, two stores with the merchandise still on the shelves...everything.

It was a spacious hotel room, even though the somewhat monastic furniture was reminiscent of the austere period of the 1950s. There was a double bed covered in woolen blankets, a table with a shaded lamp, one chair, and a dresser framed by a wood carving of the laurels of yesteryear. Glancing in the mirror, I saw a travel-weary, sweaty tourist in a blue raincoat, quite unsuited to the summer weather outside: a man with whitening stubble on his face, unshaven since leaving Prague, a bruise on the throat, and a sag in the jaw line from a recently-extracted tooth. All these made him look older than I remembered him.

From the window I could see sloping roofs, their black slate tiles gleaming in the sun under soot-stained chimneys, and the steeple of a distant church (Saint Theresa?). Down below on the broad Main Street stood a long line of cars, roof racks crowded with mattresses, suitcases, and baskets. One of T.'s five policemen was strutting around full of self-importance and trying to calm the agitated drivers.

"They're headed for the Polish border, the clerk told me," commented my wife.

"Maybe at night one can hear the river?" I thought aloud.

"Maybe," my wife said tenderly.

"I think I will shave now."

"In my honor!" she teased me.

"For who else?"

"Liar!" she protested.

WE TRUDGED ALONG THE ROAD that ran parallel to the railway, looking at the houses wedged one against another in a kind of high, defensive wall protecting the people hiding within. Despite the early afternoon hour, most of the stores were closed. I paused before an iron gate to read the names of the tenants, searching for a familiar name. I glanced up at the balconies and windows, I glanced down, disappointed. I looked at the maple trees in the park trying to remember the games of hide-and-seek we used to play with Frau Schtiasna's daughter (what was her name?), and with Grandpa. I saw the nannies staring at the aging tradesman who peeked out behind the tree so his grandson could spot him, and, triumphant in his discovery, race toward a hug.

"I saw the gentleman giving Tommy chocolates before dinner!" my nanny would say.

"Hold your tongue or you're fired!" Grandpa would retort.

I remembered Grandpa chasing me along the path, then resting on a bench, mopping his brow with a silk handkerchief, and muttering about how he had promised his doctor to take care of his heart. In the winter of 1942 Grandpa stood in line beside me on the platform at the railway station, awaiting the transport:

"If you don't show the dogs you're scared," he told me, "they'll leave you alone. Just shut your eyes and pretend that we're in the park. Remember the chocolates I used to slip you?"

"Yes, Grandpa. The taste of them is still melting in my mouth."

Once, while we were in the park we met a gypsy with a bear on a leash: Grandpa handed him a coin and asked him to make the bear dance for me, but the bear didn't want to, even though the gypsy yelled at him, jerked the chain, and beat him with a stick.

"Don't hit him!" I pleaded, when suddenly the bear reared up on his hind legs and started to grunt and growl.

"Promise not to hit him again and Grandpa'll pay you some more! Right, Grandpa?"

"Right. How much do you want for your stick?"

"That was only for fun. We're pals. He likes to dance."

I had a feeling the gypsy was lying.

"Can I pet him?"

"Sure, of course."

I went up and stroked the brown fur. The bear kneeled down and laid its head on my shoulder.

"If that bad gypsy ever hits you again," I whispered, "come and tell me. Grandpa'll call a policeman and have him put in prison."

That same night the bear visited me in my bedroom. He licked me on the cheek with a warm, welcoming tongue, and gazed at me with big, sad eyes. I got out of bed, held out my hands, and we danced together.

BY NOW MY WIFE had found a street sign, overlaid by a cardboard sticker, bearing the original name of the main street. Seeing the name raised the hair on the nape of my neck and made me feel dizzy.

"Are you all right, Tommy?"

"Not exactly, but I'll survive."

"Maybe we should find a place to drink a cup of coffee before –"

"We'll have the coffee later. Now we're going home!"

Wiping my eyes and trying to banish the black spots that suddenly seemed to overwhelm my sight like poppy seeds, I attempted to find my bearings between the buildings that separated me from what I had come for. As if by instinct, I started walking. I moved like a blind man dragged along by a guide dog, sniffing the air and trying to sense the scenery. I struggled to remember, to identify the house, but only when I stood opposite the huge building did I realize that I had reached my goal.

"Do you remember the house, Tommy?" my wife asked gently.

I shook my shoulders, ashamed to admit that for a moment I did not.

"Don't you remember the street?"

I looked at the shops and at the dark houses, desperate to find a clue.

"Don't push me, please. It will come back to me."

"Did the town change so much?"

"Not really. Now I remember the terrace, up there…and the entrance to the house."

"You were just a kid when you were forced to leave," she tried to comfort me.

"At the end of the street is the river and the bridge. On the right is the square of the municipality building." The pictures began coming back to me.

"I was sure you'd remember!"

At this point, I tried to recognize anyone among the people who were flashing curious glances at us and hurrying on their way. I wanted to stop them, to shout: "I'm Tommy H.! I was born here! Doesn't anyone remember me?!"

I yearned for somebody, anybody, to approach me, to stare at me with unbelieving eyes and exclaim: "Tommy?! Is it really you? I remember your Grandpa with the mustache and the fancy walking stick. What a grand store he had, the best in town!

"And your Papa, such a tall fellow! Walter, wasn't it? All the girls were crazy about him. He worked in the store and used to play tennis at the German Club. He hiked around the hills and waltzed with some of the girls from the best families. But only some of them because some families wouldn't let their daughters dance with a Jew. I, myself, heard the pharmacist whisper to his wife, 'If it's serious, we'll get him to convert. He doesn't look Jewish at all.' I don't think your Grandpa would ever have agreed to a priest baptizing Walter, even though he wasn't all that religious and would have done anything for his only son. But going to church, kneeling before the altar, lighting candles for the saints? That'd be too much.

"In the end, they brought Walter a bride from Poland, the daughter of a distant relative, a Jewish greengrocer with a beard down to his waist, that's the way we used to joke about them. Some people turned up their noses and said, 'like unto like.'

"You should have seen your Papa's girlfriends when little Hilde nabbed him! One of them leaped into the river and almost drowned. Lucky for her it wasn't very deep water and the coalman was crossing the bridge on his cart at the time. He jumped off and dragged her out. She was drenched to the bone and screaming 'Let me die, let me die!' They even wrote about it in the local paper. Then they had to apologize to the family and explain that the girl had simply slipped and fallen into the water. But we all knew what was what.

"Your Mama was a beauty, a little creature with coal-black braids and blazing eyes. Energetic too. Went right into the shop and won the customers' hearts. You can imagine your grandmother wasn't all that happy about customers preferring to be served by the young Frau Hilde. She soon shifted her daughter-in-law to the smaller shop. You used to have two shops, did you know that?

"So you really are Tommy! Hard to believe it. Your nanny used to wheel you around in your carriage in the park. And the dog…what was his name? Off-white with black patches, used to run alongside, wagging its tail and barking at anyone who dared approach the little prince. You've changed, you know that?"

The dog was run over a week after my father left for Palestine.

SUDDENLY I FOUND MYSELF on the pavement facing the impressive brownstone house my grandfather built, staring at it, trying to imprint every detail into my memory. I knew I'd have to give an account to my parents back home. I looked at the big shop over to the right, with two display windows and its big sign, "HABERDASHERY," and the smaller shop to the left, where my mother used to sell hats but which now sold records and tapes.

When Grandpa grew ill and wasn't able to get down the stairs, he used to sit out on that small first-floor balcony, that now boasted potted red and white petunias (I wondered who looked after them). He used to sit there counting the customers emerging from the shops. During dinner he would tug at his mustache and taunt Grandma Valli, "It seems to me that I saw more satisfied customers coming out from Hilde's shop than I did from your big one."

"If you have any complaints, I can always stay home," Grandma would reply angrily, passing an arthritic hand through her graying hairs.

I HAD BEEN INFORMED by "reliable sources" (Mama) about the tense atmosphere at home throughout the year before the outbreak of war:

"I saw Herr Fleischer," complained Grandpa, "that fellow from the German Youth Movement who walks around with a swastika on his armband, coming out with nothing. We need German clients these days."

"He wanted a wool coat, two silk shirts, and four neckties, all on credit. You know we've got this sign over the counter: 'Please don't ask for credit. A refusal often offends.'"

"You didn't give Fleischer credit?!"

Grandma seemed agitated and sent the housekeeper from the room. "Mascha, we don't need you for the moment. Go to the kitchen. I'll call you when we're ready."

When Mascha left, Grandma said, "I told him you weren't feeling well and I had to ask you about it."

"Well done. When he comes back tomorrow give him everything he asks for, and apologize. We don't want trouble with that type."

"Apologize? What for? What's happening to us, Sigmund?"

"Just do as I say, Valli."

Papa dropped his fork and stared at his parents in amazement. Mama wanted to interrupt, but Papa hinted that she shouldn't. Mama, however, who knew full well that Grandpa was very fond of her, wiped her lips with a napkin and opened her mouth.

"These German-born citizens are getting worse every day! Just this morning some German woman was asking Frau Schtiasna why she buys from the Jews. So she told her, 'They've got the fanciest hats!' She knows how to tell people off. But then the German woman screamed at her, 'When our people will be in charge here, we'll settle the account!'"

"That's all we need," Grandpa sighed. "Something's got to be done before it's too late. God Almighty, if only I was healthier and a few years younger!"

Grandpa, a sophisticated secular Jew, seldom invoked the Almighty when it came to business.

That evening the family held a lengthy gathering in the spacious living room. It had been only a few months since the Munich Pact and Kristallnacht, and Grandpa was still deeply shocked by the way in which Chamberlain and Daladier had humbled themselves before Hitler's demands and the consequent pillaging of Jewish property in Germany. He despaired of "Chattering Chamberlain," who emerged as no gentleman and broke his promises to President Benes and Foreign Minister Krofta. Grandpa Sigmund found it hard to swallow that civilized Germany was now ruled by a "band of hooligans." He regarded Hitler's rise to power as a personal insult.

"Our poor dear Czechoslovakia is captured!" he mourned in much the same way Heine had grieved over his emperor. We handed over our border fortifications, our coal mines, our steel-works, our textile and chemical industries, our forests, and our power stations. All for free, without that little Austrian sign-painter firing a single shot! Benes should have torn that Munich Pact, called up the army, and gone to war!"

Once the Germans marched into the Sudetenland, the Poles entered into T. and the surrounding areas, and the Hungarians annexed parts of Slovakia, Grandpa's condition rapidly deterio-rated. He would read all the newspapers, listen to Hitler's "historic" speeches on the radio, and silently curse Benes's successor.

"Doctor Emil has very good intentions, but he is both weak-kneed and senile."

The family was flooded with his strategic analyses: "The British and the French are deluding themselves that Hitler will be satisfied with the pound of Czech flesh and let them lie in peace in London and in Paris. Stupidity! They will pay for this betrayal. Hitler plans to conquer all of Europe, and you can't stop that with an umbrella. America could stop it, but my relatives in Washington write to me that the isolationists have Roosevelt tied down to his wheelchair. They're none too eager to sacrifice their kids for poor old Europe."

"And what about us, Sigmund?" Grandma asked.

"Wait and see. It's lucky we speak German."

"Did you read about what they're doing to the German-speaking Jews in Germany?" Mama said fervently.

"I did. I'm worried. Something's got to be done," my father said at last.

"You're right, Walter," Grandpa assured him.

At this point Grandpa sipped a glass of water and took a tranquilizer. He wanted to call Mascha to clear away the dishes, but Grandma said she had likely gone to bed and it wasn't worth waking her. Grandpa agreed, adding that Mascha was very trustworthy and that he intended to give her a raise.

A few weeks after this midnight conference, Papa set off for Palestine on a tourist visa. An ailing Grandpa, together with Grandma, Mama, and I (then barely three years old), stayed behind to guard the two shops and the house.

*   *   *

I TOOK SNAPSHOTS of the house and stores from all possible angles before crossing the street to gaze at the shop window: colorful tablecloths, a bolt of cloth, underwear, a checkered umbrella, and some leather handbags. I took a deep breath and entered the shop, my wife on my heels.

The moment I stepped in, the veil that had blurred my sight was lifted, and I could picture our shop clearly and identify the changes that the new owners had made. The cash register, sitting where Grandma's ample form once sat making sure Papa and the shop assistants were taking care of the customers, was in its usual place on a small table by the door; behind it, a mute, black telephone. From here ran a long U-shaped counter that separated the customers from the shelves. These were lined with livid-green paper reminding me of a surgeon's operating gown. A dark curtain cut off part of what once had been a much bigger shop.

There were two saleswomen. The younger wore mauve lipstick

and had shoulder-length, untidy, honey-colored hair. The elder was without makeup on her chubby face. Both eyed us with suspicion.

"Makes you feel like a shoplifter," my wife muttered.

I asked (in German) for half a dozen handkerchiefs, three linen neckties, an umbrella (for Mama), some kitchen towels, and a couple of cheap canvas shopping bags. Grandpa, who had prided himself on bringing the latest fashions from Vienna, Prague, and Warsaw, would have turned in his grave (if he had one) at the sight of the shoddy goods now on sale in his once elegant store.

The younger saleswoman piled the goods on the counter, seemingly amazed at such an extravagant shopping spree, thinking about her own salary and envying the tourists with money to burn. My wife chose a few colorful head scarves, a tablecloth, napkins, white cotton socks, some mother-of-pearl buttons, and two skeins of knitting wool (for Mama).

"That's it as far as I'm concerned. Let's go," she said.

I didn't want to leave just yet; I still wanted to finger the countertop, breathe in the dense air, and find out what lay behind that curtain. I sent my wife over to settle the account, and I continued to wander around. The elder saleswoman told the younger one to add up the bill and started to follow me, leaning slightly on the counter; it was only then that I noticed she had a slight limp.

"Would the gentleman be looking for something in particular?" She also spoke in German and sounded quite friendly.

"What have you got there?"

"Behind the curtain? Why would you be asking?"

"Just curious. I thought you might have old stock in there. My wife and I are interested in clothes from before the war." I was doubtful that an experienced saleswoman would buy such a feeble excuse, but she continued to chat nevertheless.

"Back in the fifties when my late husband and I leased this property, we were lucky enough to find boxes in the cellar with fine flannel shirts, Austrian raincoats, and English tweed jackets.

Hidden there, I suppose, by the previous owners before they ran away. God bless them for that. I'm told they were Jews. Anyway, it won't matter now if I tell you we sold the stash under the counter and made a small fortune out of it. But that was a long time ago. Nowadays we've only got cheap stuff, local products or imports from Hungary and Poland."

"Maybe you'll soon be buying from Austria and Germany?"

"There are those who do that already, like Pavel just down the street. But salaries haven't gone up, and the people…" She broke off for a moment.

"I see you staring at that curtain. I can show you what's behind it if you like. My late husband always liked to peek through the neighbors' window," she added with a giggle.

"Was there anything worth seeing?"

"Believe me, at her age I was prettier than she was. Even with that damn leg." She dragged back the curtain to reveal rows of empty shelves, a folding bed covered by a blanket, and a small table with an electric kettle, two round containers, a couple of mugs, and a box of cookies.

"This is where we make ourselves something to drink. Now and then I take a nap here when there are no customers. Renata, she lowered her voice, the girl at the counter, brings her boyfriend here in the evenings. I don't mind. They're young, they're in love, and they've got nowhere else to go."

I had noticed a lengthy wooden board leaning against the wall behind the bed.

"And what is this?" I inquired.

"Ah, that. Would you mind bending over and coming behind the counter?"

By now my wife was wondering what I was up to.

"It's a leftover from the old shop. When we had a cold winter and coal got expensive, I wanted to chop it up for firewood, but my late husband never let me. 'Wait and see, sweetie,' he'd say. He always called me that when he wanted something. 'One day there'll come some crazy American who'll pay its weight in gold for that sign.'"

"Sign?"

"Turn it around, take a look."

My wife lent me a hand in turning over the heavy board. The letters hadn't faded. The shop's name, "THE GENTLEMAN" appeared on either side in English, along with illustrations of socks, shirts, and starched collars, a jacket, gloves, belts, and a leather wallet. And below this the name: Sigmund H. & Son. I gazed at it with adoring eyes, biting my lips.

"They knew how to paint signs in those days," I finally blurted out. "D'you mind if I take a picture?"

"Please do. Maybe you would like to buy it for a hundred dollars?" She seemed to be speaking to herself.

"It's too heavy to carry," I whispered. "Just a picture for our collection."

"Why not? I will probably just burn it this winter." I didn't respond. Instead I turned to my wife, "What a pity Father isn't here to take a look at it."

"Pardon me, what language are you speaking?" the saleswoman interjected.

"Hebrew."

"That's the language of the Jews, isn't it?"

"The Israelis."

"Isn't that the same thing?"

"More or less. Many thanks madam. Can I add something to the bill?" My wallet was already halfway out of my pocket.

"No, no, sir. It's quite enough what I've made on the sale already. We don't get customers like you every day. You could give it to Renata, she's saving up every crown for her wedding. Will you and your wife be continuing on this evening to A. or going back on the night train to Prague?"

"We're staying the night at the hotel here in T."

"When will I learn to keep my mouth shut?" she mumbled to herself as she replaced the curtain and limped her way back to the desk. I handed the younger woman a hundred-crown note and bid her farewell (in Czech). My wife was waiting outside with the packages. On my way out I noticed the saleswoman with the limp calling someone on the phone.

"So now they know I'm here."

"You sound happy about it."

"Happy and scared."

"Who can do anything to us?"

"Dunno. Just feeling it in my stomach. Like Mama. How about buying a tape in her shop?"

"As you wish."

\*   \*   \*

IN THE RECORD STORE the loudspeakers beat out rock and disco rhythms, and giant posters on the walls depicted the Beatles, Elvis, and Dalida. An exhibition case displayed rare discs of the classics alongside tapes and CDs of current hits. I looked around, searching for Mama, who would use any moment, when there were no customers, to try on a new hat and admire herself in the mirror. Or she could be seen frantically opening box after box serving some stubborn lady who insisted on finding a unique hat to amaze her girlfriends and arouse gazes from the playboys on the street.

"I got some cassettes of Czechoslovakian folk music, a Beethoven symphony conducted by Toscanini, and Dvořák's *Slovenian Dances*. I paid for them already," my wife told me. There wasn't much left to do but say goodbye and head outside.

"Let's buy some food at that Pavel place and get back to the hotel. You can take a look at the house tomorrow."

"I have to see it now."

"Do you mind going alone?"

"No. Go to that delicatessen. We'll meet here at the shop in another fifteen minutes. If I'm not back, call the cops."

"That's not funny."

"I'm not trying to be funny."

"Maybe I'll come up with you all the same? I promised your mother to take care of you."

"She must have said, 'Don't tell Tommy, but…'"

"How did you guess that?"

"I slept with Mama on the same bench for twenty-two months in Bergen-Belsen. I can read her thoughts."

\*　　\*　　\*

BEFORE MOVING TO T., Grandpa used to live with his family in a small mining town not far from A. He paid a bargain price there for a miserable clothing store, whose owner had gone bankrupt, and redecorated the place. He put in a show window that displayed suits and dresses brought from the big cities, and turned the ruin into a goldmine. Soon the wives of the clerks at the mine, the engineers, and local officials stopped buying in A. and started buying regularly from the Jew. Many of the locals became envious of this successful salesman who could speak German, Czech, and Polish. The one who kept all his promises and was a stylish dresser invited to all fashionable homes, even to the castle of the Baron Schpitz. The aging aristocrat would consult my grandfather on investments and dealing with troublesome workers.

"They want to cut down on their hours and get more wages, the rascals! Want me to put good ponies down the mines to drag the coal trucks!"

"The baron should treat them gently. They're desperate. They've got nothing to lose but their tuberculosis."

"To hell with them! I'm told those bastards meet in secret and then hand out Bolshevik pamphlets."

"It's hard to stop a wheel running downhill after it's broken off from the wagon."

"What wheel? What wagon? Sigmund, don't talk to me in parables."

"Just don't rush things, sir. Take it easy on the reins." Baron Schpitz waved aside Grandpa's advice with a trembling hand.

"I'm not afraid of the mob!" (He coughed in a paroxysm that blew out his monocle.) "This is just between you and me, a letter from his Excellency, the Emperor Franz Joseph. He promises me a troop of Hussars, swords-drawn, at the mines, to teach those rebels a lesson they'll never forget!"

Afterwards, the Austrian baron and the Jewish merchant exchanged opinions about the opera *The Bartered Bride,* which they had both seen in Vienna, and settled down to a game of cards.

NOW AND THEN, when cold and hunger struck the area, Grandpa would hire a peasant with a horse-drawn sled and visit the poverty-stricken miners buried beneath the snow and hand out warm clothing and food. The widows and orphans, seeing the trader in his fur coat, saw him as something like Santa Claus. The women kissed his hand (Sigmund did not like that) and wished him a long life: he and his blessed wife and little Walter. There were others who refused to take charity from him.

"We're the ones who crawl through the tunnels like moles; it is we who breathe dust and spit blood. And this Jew, who crucified our Savior, eats white bread all week long and lives like a king!"

WHEN THE HEIR TO THE THRONE, Archduke Ferdinand, was assassinated at Sarajevo, Grandpa was drafted. The war was supposed to be over within six weeks with an Imperial Victory. Unfortunately, against all the prophecies of the distinguished General Staff, it dragged out for four bloodstained years ending in the dissolution of the vast Austro-Hungarian Empire.

In 1914, Grandpa Sigmund was thirty-two years old, a successful businessman, a man with connections in the mid-level echelons of government, but was physically frail due to an occasionally unstable heartbeat. The recruiting board that examined him was impressed by his appearance and achievements and considered sending him to the officer's training course. However, since they had already registered three Jews for such a privilege, Grandpa was assigned to the offices of the military surgeon in A., a former gynecologist whose main task was to treat the mistresses of staff officers for venereal diseases and occasionally authorize abortions. This was a fairly cushy job, which enabled Grandpa to take frequent leaves of absence and help Grandma run the shop.

During the war years, Grandpa learned a certain amount of medical practice. While the doctor was away somewhere in the Tatra hills with his fiancée, Grandpa would be down there prescribing aspirins or enemas, and signing and rubber-stamping recommendations for amputees just out of hospital to receive the Iron Cross (second or third class). There was, however, one thing that bothered him: his grey-green uniform was poorly tailored from inferior material and was itchy. He hated it. With little help from the quartermaster's stores, he ordered a decent uniform from his personal tailor. One can imagine the way in which doctors and medics in the army clinic goggled at Grandpa in his magnificent uniform with its corporal stripes on the sleeves.

"You can't get away with that!" screamed the gynecologist.

"Every costume has its cost." Grandpa replied. "Drop in at the tailor and ask him to make you one. The bill's already paid."

"A uniform like that ought to have a medal of some sort," winked the Kapitan.

"Leave the medals to those who choke on poison gas in the trenches and who go over the top with fixed bayonets trampling over the corpses of their comrades. I'm no hero." "We're also doing our duty, corporal!" the Kapitan hissed, turning back to deal with a girl who had sprained an ankle dancing the Czardash with an officer.

One day Grandpa was summoned to headquarters and informed that the doctor had recommended him for a medal of distinguished service. He didn't really want it, but he understood that it would be better not to appear ungrateful. And so, at an impressive parade-ground ceremony, there was Grandpa Sigmund puffing out his chest (his heart skipping a beat at the same moment) while the doctor pinned on the medal, embraced him fondly, and patted him on the shoulder.

From then on, whenever Grandpa came home on leave, the neighbors would salute him with respect. Once he noticed their admiring glances, Grandpa adopted a slight limp, bought himself an ivory-topped cane, and got into the habit of muttering, "Just my luck that the army sawbones didn't have his saw that day."

Gossip soon spread among the locals about Grandpa's acts of heroism. On hearing these stories he would tug at his clipped mustache, cursing the Kapitan-doctor who had brought such shame on him. In the end he couldn't stand it any longer, and he hid his medal in a trunk, reserving it for possible future use.

TOWARD THE END OF THE WAR when the rusting hoops of the Great Empire were loosening and the oppressed nations were raising their bowed heads and flags, there were also riots at the coal mines between A. and K. Frustrated miners grabbed spades and sledgehammers and marched on the baron's fortified castle. A faithful guard in the watchtower who happened to be armed with a shotgun blasted off a few rounds of birdshot into the advancing mob, wounding a few of them. The miners halted in confusion, huddled around their injured comrades, and decided on a different, more vulnerable target. They set off for David's tavern, on the outskirts of town. There they proceeded to drain the barrels of Yash and beer and beat up the Jewish bartender.

David, who had escaped by a miracle, was able to warn the rest of the Jews of the forthcoming pogrom. During their improvised rampage the miners rounded up and drove off the horses and cows they found grazing on the common. Armed with stolen pitchforks, they ambushed the local postman who happened to ride by on his bicycle. The mail scattered, and the old man's cap, bearing the insignia of the Imperial Post Office, was taken by the rebels. They proceeded to argue over who would wear the cap and who would get to ride the bike. The vast amounts of Yash that had been consumed started going to their heads: they began to sing of the river's slow flow and of a young maiden picking the flowers of the field. They sang haunting melodies that fill the heart with feelings of longing and indeed induced tears in some of the more emotional among them, who began to beat their breasts mourning their miserable fate.

Some arrived on horseback, some running alongside, some staggering, falling and getting up again. The rebel miners reached the town square and were joined by their wives and children. Awaiting them on the steps of the church, the local priest stood grasping the silver crucifix and was flanked by two novices who stood by him like cherubim.

"Be not afraid, my children, the Lord is with us!" he soothed the innocent pupils beside him, who were still unaware of the degree of danger.

"Holy Father, that's our horse!" cried one of the novices, and at his shrill whistle of command, the horse threw its rider and galloped toward the steps of the church.

Such an apocalyptic vision, a howling riderless horse and a demonic mob armed with blazing torches and pitchforks, seemed to unnerve the Holy Father. Gathering his cloak, he fled back into the precincts of the church, followed closely by his novices who swiftly barred the door. The horse remained outside, whinnying and snorting from the head of the steps at the crowd below.

The two policemen posted to guard the town hall affixed bayonets and then read the riot act, ordering the mob to disperse. However, as the tide of inflamed miners surged forward, they both beat a hasty strategic retreat into the courtyard in search of reinforcements and vowed to hold out to the last man.

The starving women were the ones who urged their husbands to plunder the shops: men and boys smashed the locks and raised the steel shutters. Then everyone flooded in, stuffing and stealing saucepans, frying pans, and soup plates. From the neighboring shop they took rolls of cloth and items of clothing; from the next shop, boots and shoes (in haste, it is said, someone took two left boots); and from the grocer's, sacks of sugar, salt, and dried peas, cans of cooking oil, rounds of cheese, whole salamis, bottles of vinegar, whatever could be stowed away in a shawl, pressed into the hungry hands of children, or dragged on the back for a getaway before law and order could be restored. Once they had finished off the merchandise, they took the chairs, the counters, the shelves, the mirrors, and the oil lamps. Whatever they couldn't take away, they smashed to pieces. Grandpa and Grandma's shop was also looted.

Once the shouting died down, people began to drift off to their homes, clutching their newly-won possessions, looking forward to the daybreak shift in the mines in order not to lose a day's wages (God forbid). But there were still some groups of miners left in the square with little else to do. At this point someone proposed looting the homes of the Jews, "who hide their gold in their pillowcases and under their mattresses." Quite a number of those present were against this, claiming that the Jews had lived in the town for generations as good neighbors. There were others who accused the rich Jews of collaborating with the Austrian rulers. After loud and long debates a small crowd of hotheaded people turned toward the Jewish homes.

There were Jews who found refuge with Christian neighbors and peeked through the windows to watch their other neighbors plundering their houses. There were some who grabbed iron bars and attacked the drunken rioters, only to be felled and trampled by the screaming mob. Grandma Valli hid my father under the bed and stationed herself beside the door: a tall threatening figure with prominent cheekbones and an aquiline nose. People glanced at her, undecided. Some of them slunk away with downcast eyes. Suddenly, the local blacksmith's apprentice shoved her aside.

"Wipe your boots, boy!" she almost shouted at him.

"Quite a palace!" he sneered. "Come in comrades, don't hang about there in the doorway. First come, first serve!"

Grandma could only stand there and watch them flood in, ransack every room, rip up chairs sending the upholstery flying. They snatched up the silver candlesticks, the holy candelabra, the carpets and rugs, coats, towels, sheets, Grandpa's shirts and long underwear. One woman even wrapped a corset around her waist and entertained the looters with an improvised belly-dance before realizing that she might be missing her chance to get something better worth taking. They went on, swarming into the kitchen, grabbing jars of jam and pickles from the larder. And just when two were squabbling over who saw the coffee grinder first, a neighbor broke in screaming her head off:

"Shame on you, good citizens! What's become of you? Have you forgotten everything your good parents ever taught you? Our Herr Sigmund battled for our homeland as a hero. He was even awarded a medal! And here you are looting his home and humiliating his wife? Have you forgotten how he used to bring you clothing and blankets for Christmas? You used to call him Santa Claus. Drop everything you've got there and get out of this house! And go to church on Sunday and confess and beg absolution from the Holy Father. Where is the child? You surely haven't harmed little Walter?"

Papa crawled out from under the bed, clutching Grandma's apron strings, gaping at the assembled "guests." Grandma drew him to her bosom and murmured, "Don't be afraid."

Gradually, the men began to drop their loot and slip away. Women angrily ripped toys from the clutching hands of their weeping offspring. Throwing a backward glance at the well-kept but by now almost empty home, they slunk off like scolded children from a classroom.

Our brave neighbor was more than hospitable: "Come my dear, you can sleep at our place tonight. We have plenty of bed clothing."

"I am most grateful, but we shall lock our doors and remain at home. Sigmund will never forget how you protected us, how you saved our lives."

"I would have never believed such things of upright Christians."

"You have seen for yourself. It's possible."

"What can we do to help? Don't hesitate to ask."

"Could your husband find a horse and ride to A. to tell the corporal about all this?"

"I can ask him when he's awake and sober. He, too, God forgive him, was with the mob at David's tavern."

The following day Grandpa rode into the small town at the head of a ten-man patrol of armed cavalry. People who encountered him on his way hid in their homes. When he arrived, Grandpa embraced both his wife and his little son. Then, after estimating the damage and checking that the priceless Gottlieb oil painting, that concealed a safe containing coins and jewelry, was still in place, he heaved a sigh of relief.

"Don't you worry."

"Was I complaining?" Grandma seemed insulted.

"The main thing is that Walter and you are safe."

It was then that Grandpa discerned a certain glint in Walter's eyes: this was the first time his son had ever dared to stand by his Mama. Maybe Walter thought they had both been abandoned, that he, the breadwinner, who also supported his poor sisters, had let them down?

"Would you like to ride on my horse?" he said, trying to tempt his boy.

"No."

"Well, maybe later. We'll ride around the square like two troopers."

Grandpa stayed for three days to conduct house-to-house searches. He managed to retrieve some of the stolen goods, but never found the silver candlesticks or the silver goblet that were family heirlooms. Now and then he would stop a miner in the middle of the street and order him to take off the poplin shirt he was wearing with Grandpa's monogram. The poor fellow would mumble an apology, strip off the shirt, and run for his life in his ragged, stained undergarments. When his three-day leave was up and Grandpa had to return to the base at A., Grandma informed him that she was taking the child and moving to her parents' home in the country. Grandpa Sigmund, unused to accepting orders, made no objection this time.

"Go back to your family until generals stop their saber-rattling and shake hands like good little boys. Drink fresh milk (Grandma's father was a milkman), eat fresh fruits and vegetables, and get a bit of sunshine. And you, Walter, practice your riding and the multiplication table. I don't want to be ashamed of you!"

WHEN HE WAS RELEASED from the army Grandpa sold both the house and the shop.

"I'm not prepared to live among thieves!" he proclaimed before his acquaintances, who couldn't understand why a successful tradesman should ever want to leave them.

Grandpa invested his money in war surplus: opportunistic quartermasters were only too happy to get rid of outdated ruins piling up in their warehouses, and were rewarded by a handsome commission paid directly into their own pockets. Grandpa sold this junk to a steel foundry in urgent need of raw material, making a small fortune along the way. One day he turned up in a pony-trap to inform Grandma that he'd been offered a vacant plot of land in the center of T. and had half a mind to buy it. Grandma, who knew her husband quite well, was convinced that he had either decided, or had actually bought it already.

"Should I start packing?" she asked.

"Take it easy, Valli. Don't rush. You've got a couple of hours' time. The carts and the porters won't be here until tomorrow. I've rented an apartment in T. We'll be living there until they finish building the house."

On their way to T. Grandpa gave Walter a multiplication exam and scolded him on every mistake: "A trader must know how to make accounts."

"The child's nervous," Grandma protested, "and besides, who knows, maybe he wants to be an artist?"

"I've seen his sketches. He won't be a Rembrandt, that's for sure. D'you want to see the plans for the house?"

"You have plans already?"

"But of course!" Grandpa was gloating by now. "By the best architect in A.! I told him, 'Spare no expense. I want my home to be –'"

"Sigmund, aren't you overdoing it? Why show off? Who needs a three-story house and two shops down below?"

"You're still the same Valli, always your father's daughter."

"And I mean to stay that way."

"The whole world is changing, dearest. Czechoslovakia, Poland, Yugoslavia, they're all independent nations now."

"What was so bad for them as part of the Empire?"

"Every people wants its own flag, its own parliament, its own army, its own currency."

"So…who are we, the Jews?"

"Czechs, of course. German speakers and believers in the Mosaic faith."

"Believers?"

"It's a personal matter. Walter was circumcised just to please your family."

"And if it had been up to you?"

"Valli, Valli. Don't be provocative. The child can hear."

"So let him. Let him learn to look the world in the face and ask questions! For me that's more important than the multiplication tables and riding a horse with straight back. That mob that robbed our house reminded him that he's a Jew."

"That's just why we're moving to T. There's a better kind of people there, more educated, more tolerant. There's a German high school there, a sports club, an amateur theatrical society, and people who can afford to waste their money on fancy clothes. I've already thought about the sign for our shop: It will read 'THE GENTLE-MAN,' in English! Then the Czechs, the Germans, and the Poles can't have any complaints. Don't you think it's brilliant?"

"I don't like these brilliant ideas of yours."

"Valli! Walter is eavesdropping!"

"As far as I'm concerned, let him be an artist!"

\*　　\*　　\*

MY WIFE HAD BEEN swallowed up by the delicatessen on the corner of the street, and here I was, standing hesitantly before daring to set a foot inside. After I turned on the light in the hallway, I was confronted by a marble tablet with the names of my grandfather, the architect, and the year in which the house was built. It was damaged: someone had apparently attempted to erase the words, but the names engraved in stone had withstood the vandal's chisel.

I ascended the staircase, which was worn by age, stroking the rounded wooden banister, sensing the flakes of faded varnish. My nanny, Hela, used to carry me down here from the upstairs apartment, give me a warm hug, and then I would gaze through the windows at the fruit trees in the backyard. Now I could see the grey roof of an asbestos shed that took the place of the apple trees that had fallen. When I had learned how to run, I used to rush down these stairs accompanied by Grandpa's warnings:

"Hela, watch the child, make sure he doesn't fall down!"

Arriving upstairs I could see that the five-room apartment, once occupied by our entire family (the young couple to the right, Grandpa and Grandma to the left), had been divided into two. I read the Czech name on the label and rang the bell. No answer. I tried again, placing my ear to the door and trying to discern any movement within. I waited for a moment and then started pounding the door as if I were a landlord demanding immediate entry.

To my left a door was opened warily, and a woman squinted at me with a suspicious look. I moved toward her but she slammed the door in my face. I tapped gently on her door and could hear her breathing heavily, holding back a cough.

"Who are you here for?"

A simple, yet embarrassing question, which forced me to drop my mask and confess my identity to this anonymous woman behind the locked door.

"I was born in this neighboring apartment."

After a moment of hesitation, the woman finally unlocked her door, blocking the entry with her large frame.

"I don't understand German," she claimed in Czech.

Summoning almost every word I could recall from childhood (in Czech and Polish), I did my best to explain that before the war my grandparents had lived in her apartment. She looked at me with narrowed, frightened eyes, clutching her doorpost, and stubbornly claimed that she didn't understand what I was talking about. I was sure that she had understood and knew exactly who I was. I reckoned that she was scared I might come back tomorrow with a lawyer or a government clerk (from the Department of Abandoned Property) and suddenly whip out eviction orders. I tried to calm her down, to allay her fears. I explained that I had come from far away, from Jerusalem, and asked her for permission to enter, just for a few moments. I told her I had played here as a child with an electric train set. I glimpsed a spark of goodwill in that square-set face, but it was immediately cut off by a cough. She continued to block the doorway.

"*Nein, nein!* My husband is not at home. It is *verboten* to let in strangers. Is *verboten.*"

Some of her words had slipped out in German. Now she seemed to be biting her tongue as if afraid to be punished for lying.

*I was so close.* I was so close to that room that had housed the sofa where Grandpa used to sit, bouncing me up and down on his knee and singing about the horse galloping over fences and over rocks. I glared at the woman. She wore a somber dress with her hair pinned up clumsily behind her head. She looked to me like a kind of fearsome schoolteacher who whacks her pupils over the fingers with a ruler and pinches the pink cheeks of her prettiest schoolgirls. I wanted simply to shove her aside and force my way in, but her stubbornness (or my good manners or inherent cowardice), made me uneasy, and somehow I gave way.

Could I just take a look?"

"*Verboten!*" Then she closed the door.

STANDING OPPOSITE those locked doors I could suddenly see Grandpa Sigmund coming home from his work at the Judenrat in the Rzeszow Ghetto.

"Got something good for you, Tommy," he whispered, stroking my lean cheek with his thin, frozen fingers.

"You've brought some bread?"

"Better than bread."

"Sugar lumps?"

"Even better!"

"There's nothing better than that."

"Good tidings. You're the first to know!"

"Good tidings?"

"The Judenrat has been informed by the Gestapo that the certificates Walter sent from Palestine have arrived. You and your mother have been saved!"

"It's a pity you didn't bring any bread." Grandpa chuckled as he patted my head.

"You are still a kid."

I never asked him: What about you, Grandpa? And Grandma Bluma (my mother's mother), and my cousin Ruthy? To this day I can't forgive myself for only thinking about my stomach.

*    *    *

AS I DRAGGED MYSELF up another floor, I was overtaken by my wife.

"What's up with you, Tommy? I've been waiting for over ten minutes at the shop window. I almost called the police. You look awful, are you all right? Did you see the apartment?"

"I feel awful. No, I didn't."

"I bought a lot of things."

"That's good. Did you get any…sugar lumps?"

"Why do you ask? You never take sugar."

"That's right. Forget about it. I want to try and see the upstairs apartment. I could hear kids playing up there."

"I'm coming with you."

The apartment had once been the home of the chief engineer of the local brewery whose beer was famous throughout Central Europe. He was a pedantic middle-aged German who lived in the spacious apartment with his much younger wife. They didn't have any children of their own, and the wife, whose name was Gisela, asked my grandfather to let her play hostess to myself and my nanny. Grandpa wasn't all that enthusiastic about the idea, but being eager for me to learn to speak proper German, he finally agreed, but only after Gisela promised not to stuff me with sweets.

She later broke that promise by feeding me chocolates. I would undergo intensive mouthwash before going back downstairs. Frau Gisela would read me *Grimm's Fairy Tales* and *Max and Moritz*. She would play puppet shows with me and whisper in my ear that I was her baby.

Once, when I innocently rode my hobby-horse into the engineer's study, Frau Gisela leaped from her seat and thrust me out of the door.

"Never go into Wolfgang's study. Never, ever!"

I had not been used to a scolding from my "aunty," and I promptly burst into tears. Gisela tried to comfort me, but I went on bawling and ran back home. Grandpa, who had apparently heard all the fuss, was waiting for me in the doorway.

"Did anybody dare lay a hand on you?"

I told him that Frau Gisela had yelled at me because I had entered the engineer's study.

"What did you see there?"

I was only about three years old, and it was hard for me to describe in detail what was there. I had glimpsed radios and wiring (aerials as it transpired). Grandpa listened carefully and reached his own conclusions. Later that evening he summoned Grandma Valli and Mama (Papa was already in Palestine), and revealed that for several months he had been hearing strange noises emanating from the upper floor. He was now convinced that the engineer was operating a radio transmitter and spying for the German enemy. Mama said that they should inform the police. Grandpa rejected this suggestion. In his opinion, the Germans had their men in key positions within the Polish administration, and leaks of this sort could only lead to "unpleasantness."

"Better to keep quiet. We're German speakers. Walter studied at a German high school. I served in the Austrian army with a medal to prove it. I hope they will treat us as Germans and not make any trouble for us."

"Ever the optimist!" Grandma exclaimed. "We're losing clients all the time. Only yesterday I had some German brat in there talking rudely."

"Why didn't you call me?"

Grandma sighed and ignored the question. "I know it is getting worse from day to day. I may have my delusions, but I've also got a plan. Trust Sigmund! I'm just waiting for a signal from Palestine."

When anti-Semitic provocations increased, Frau Gisela sneaked into Mama's hat shop for a tête-à-tête in the back room.

"Dear Madame Hilde, I'm here even though Wolfgang forbade me to set foot in your shop and warned me against being seen speaking to you on the street. We had a big argument about it. Maybe you heard us. He was even hinting that I might not be a pure Aryan, that my grandmother's grandmother might have been Jewish! Me…from the aristocracy of Heidelberg! And all this just because I care for you and particularly for Tommy. Wolfgang curses the Jews when he thinks I can't hear him. I don't let him do that in my presence, Hilde, may I call you that?"

"But of course, Frau Gisela!"

"Just call me Gisela. The German army will soon march into T. I know it from reliable sources. Tell this to your father-in-law. And for God's sake, get out of here before it's too late. I've got to go now, any minute Wolfgang will be back from his 'Teutonic Committee' meeting."

Mama passed on the warning to Grandpa, who told her to keep quiet; he then began to get anxious: "It seems Walter can't get hold of the damn certificates for all of us. After all, Palestine needs young people who'll work the land and work in the factories, not old fogies with one foot in the grave."

"Sigmund, you're barely sixty!" said Mama. "You're a man of property, with experience in business."

"Tell that to the British, and to the Jewish Agency in Jerusalem."

Summing up the debate, Grandpa declared his intention of moving the family to a distant holiday resort in Poland.

"We'll rent a few rooms in a peasant cottage and wait until it all blows over. The Germans will never get that far."

ABOUT A MONTH before the Germans invaded Poland, Mama and I were strolling down the road toward the bridge. I used to enjoy watching the waters and looking at the gendarmes in their booth looking just like toy soldiers. Opposite us, arm-in-arm, we could see the German engineer and his wife. When she saw us, Frau Gisela broke away from her husband and hurried over, ignoring his peremptory order to return.

"Go over to the patisserie and take a strudel and a coconut cake, I'll be with you in a moment."

"This is extremely embarrassing!"

"I just want to say hello to Tommy."

"I'll wait three minutes. If you're not there by then…"

"You'll report on me to the Gestapo? Don't forget, Heidrich is a good friend of my brother."

Herr Engineer clicked his heels and vanished into the pastry shop, and Frau Gisela whispered urgently to Mama, "I really don't know what's come over my husband. He's always been so polite and considerate, but now he seems to be infected by this hatred of Jews as if it were some kind of fatal disease. Tell me what to do, Hilde. No, on second thought, don't. Wolfgang is my problem, I'll solve it myself. What does Walter write from Palestine?"

"So far we haven't heard from him. Maybe the mail has been delayed."

"Why are you still here? The war will break out in a few days. Everything is ready. The German Panzers will crush the Polish cavalry, the Czechs won't put up any sort of fight. There's my husband in the shop doorway, he must be furious."

Frau Gisela suddenly bent over to retie one of my shoelaces.

"Poor little Tommy!" She muttered before straightening up and taking Mama's hand.

"Wolfgang's going to make a scene as soon as we get home, but I don't care! If you need anything, come to see me when he's out at work. Please don't hesitate."

"You're very kind, Frau Gisela."

"For you, just Gisela, always."

* * *

THE SECOND DOOR was opened on the first knock by a young slim suntanned woman, her brown hair swept back into a ponytail. Her T-shirt and shorts gave her a girlish appearance, although the slight creases at the corners of her mouth betrayed a greater maturity and self-confidence, and perhaps some inner scar that for a moment escaped my roving eye. She seemed a little surprised to see us, but was quite pleasant as she asked us which family we were looking for. My failure downstairs prompted me to say we were looking for the Paliweczes. She had never heard of them. I asked her whether she spoke German or English. She replied in a good English that at school they had learned Russian, and some English.

"Jan and I both studied English with a private tutor, and from Radio Prague's 'Third Program,' that's to say, the Voice of America."

Two little freckle-faced girls who looked like four-year-old twins were clinging to her shapely legs, demanding in chorus to be introduced to this new "aunt and uncle." I told them our names and they burst out in peals of laughter. Their young mother shushed them and then, seeing that we both looked a bit weary and weighed down with parcels, introduced herself as Anna and invited us in for a glass of tea.

"My husband will soon be back from the garage, maybe he knows the Paliweczes."

"How do we get out of this one?" whispered my wife.

"But now we're in!"

ANNA LED US to a spacious kitchen furnished with table and chairs and put a kettle on the gas stove. I stole a glance through the open door into the living room.

"Nice place you have here," I ventured.

"Part luck, part influence. Under the communists the rent was almost nothing. Nowadays, with the costs of electricity, water, and public transport all going up, we may have to pay double the rent. I'm not sure we'll be able to afford it for long, despite the fact that Jan works overtime and I've got a part-time job as an instructor."

My wife rifled through our shopping bags and produced some marzipan. She asked Anna if she might give a few pieces to the twins.

"They remind me of our grandchildren," she said.

"You, a grandmother?" Our hostess seemed amazed. Looking at the twins, she said, "One for each of you, little chatterboxes, and don't forget to say thank you."

"Did you get this at Pavel's?"

"Yes. Take a bit yourself."

"Thanks a lot. I'll just go and make the tea."

"Could I take a look around your living room?" I asked.

"Help yourself, but try and ignore the mess! I let the girls play and watch TV in there until it's time for Jan to come home."

The twins perched themselves on my wife's knees and gabbled away in Czech, which she answered with smiles and nods. I stole my way into the living room: the parquet floor seemed to be gleaming and undamaged. The tall windows that overlooked the street below were bordered by airy lemon-yellow curtains fluttering in a welcome evening breeze. There was a set of two armchairs and a sofa in flowered upholstery arranged along the wall, and a small set of bookshelves next to the television: a selection of whodunits and sci-fi in English, novels by Capek, Kundera, Hrabal, and Skvorecky, as well as Havel's *Letters to Olga,* an English–Czech dictionary, and photo albums of the twins. A huge poster reproduction of Picasso's *Guernica* covered most of the door leading to a bedroom, which used to be just over my parent's room. I wanted to cross that threshold, but was hesitant about abusing my welcome. Instead I went back into the kitchen.

My wife was singing Israeli folk songs to the children and talking to Anna about Jerusalem. As I sipped my glass of strong tea, I contemplated the fact that I was actually seated above my childhood room. Only the floor, covered with graying linoleum, separated me from the place where my cot had stood with the grinning clown doll.

A knock on the door reawakened me to present-day T. Anna hurried to the door.

"Jan? Did you forget your keys?"

It was the downstairs neighbor, the woman who now occupied my grandparents' apartment. She gestured toward me as if I were Judas Iscariot and addressed our hostess in a torrent of viperous whispering. My wife dropped the twins from her lap and rose decisively to her feet. The two little girls seemed upset by this sudden change of attitude.

"Hang on," I muttered, "I'm not running away."

"Neither am I. I just wanted to be near you."

Anna was posing a question; the neighbor was still haranguing her, shaking an accusing finger. I couldn't follow exactly what was being said, but there seemed to be a strong difference of opinion. It ended up with a scream that sounded like "You'll live to regret it!" after which the neighbor was gone, slamming the door behind her.

The young mother returned to the kitchen and took the frightened twins onto her lap.

"Please sit down. You are my guests. Nobody's going to drive you out."

We sat down again, slightly uneasy, but Anna did her best to smooth the ruffled waters.

"I hear that you were born in the apartment downstairs. Does the house belong to your family?"

"That's correct," I admitted, and noticed a cloud come over her tanned brow.

"How does it feel to come back like a tourist?"

"Strange and embarrassing when you run into a neighbor like yours."

"That one used to be one of the Reddest of the Reds. Everyone used to be scared of her. She'd come to borrow an egg and she'd check out who was visiting, what we were reading, and what wavelength the radio was tuned to. Now she sucks up to me and offers to baby-sit. Thinks I'll forgive the past!" Anna hesitated for a moment. "You don't intend to move us out of here, do you?"

"Good heavens, no! I just wanted to have a look at the place."

"The other neighbors downstairs are away on vacation, so you won't be able to see your apartment. A pity."

"Yes, I'm disappointed."

"Why don't you stay for supper?"

"That's very kind of you, but…"

"No buts, I can do mushroom omelets. We still have some of yesterday's Knedelichki that I can warm up, and now you'll be able to meet Jan. He's a great guy, got arrested once for making fun of Brezhnev. Said Brezhnev staggered around like a bear with Parkinson's disease. He was lucky that some of the party functionaries used to have their limousines fixed at the garage where he works and that they testified that Jan must have been drunk at the time, that he was a good Stachanovite worker who knew full well that Brezhnev could run like Emil Zatopek! Apart from that, I'm dying to hear all about Israel. You're always in the news."

It wasn't easy to refuse an invitation to dine in the company of a young Czech family and it was even less easy to refuse the offer of local Knedelichki (perhaps with sweet-and-sour dill sauce?), but I felt it was time to go. I was exhausted and had seen enough for one day. Were I to go on sitting here in this warm and welcoming kitchen, eyeing this charming hostess, the spell might vanish. So I simply made our excuses, shook her hand, expressed our gratitude, and gathered up our belongings. My wife patted the twins' curly heads and left them the rest of the marzipan. Just as we were in the doorway, Anna's clear voice stabbed me in the back:

"Tell me, when you said you were looking for 'Paliwecz,' the name rang a bell. Wasn't that the bartender who was always sober in "Good Soldier Schweik"?

"I plead guilty, milady."

"In that case, we'll settle for probation. But please, don't try anything on us. We spent years in a runaround from office to office before we got this place."

"We're not like that," said my wife as she embraced Anna.

AS WE WENT DOWNSTAIRS, I paused before the door of "our" apartment in silent anger, feeling that this barred door would never be opened to us.

Out on the street we took a deep breath and linked arms. Both of our shops were already closed, their show windows illuminated by glaring neon.

"Maybe we'll try to find Frau Schtiasna?"

"I'm tired, Tommy, and you also need a good rest."

We walked along for a while, each of us sunk in our own thoughts.

"I noticed that you couldn't take your eyes off that young woman."

"I don't know what you are talking about."

My wife suddenly stopped, producing a bottle of Slivovitz from which I took a healthy swig.

"Let me have a go at it."

"Since when do you drink?"

"As of now. Wow, that's fierce! How can you drink this stuff?"

"I'm a Czech, have you forgotten? When I was only one year old an uncle took me to the tavern and ordered sausages, sauerkraut, and a stein of beer, just for me. There's a family legend that claims I finished off the beer, licked my chops, belched, and asked for more."

"I prefer orange juice."

"I'll squeeze a few for you when we get back to Jerusalem."

"I'm homesick already."

"T. was once my home."

"I know, Tommy."

WE MARCHED TOWARD the hotel at a military pace, ignoring the buildings, the few cars on the streets, and the people taking their dogs out for an evening stroll. We halted at the hotel's entryway, and then went in by the side entrance, groping our way through the darkened dining room to the corridor that led to the out-of-service elevator.

The balding receptionist greeted us with a "good evening" that sounded somewhat chilly. Up in our room we filled the bathtub with hot water and washed off the dirt of the day. We then set ourselves down on our beds and gorged ourselves on Coca-Cola, buttered rolls, a sliver of Danish cheese, and pickled cucumbers. For dessert we wolfed down a whole bar of Swiss white milk chocolate.

Through the open window we could hear the cars edging forward and stopping with a screech of brakes, the shouts of protesting drivers, and the hoarse replies of the solitary traffic cop that still hadn't finished his shift. After dinner, we went down to the lobby. The receptionist was watching a soccer match on television, but nevertheless heaved himself out of his armchair in order to be "at our service."

"Can I make a direct-dial call from here to Israel?"

"Direct dialing works only on incoming calls. Write down the number and the area code and I'll order the call from the exchange at A."

"How long will it take?"

"Depends on the person on duty. Pity we can't slip her a dollar down the line."

Possibly oversensitive, I seemed to perceive an anti-Semitic undertone in his joviality. About half an hour later I was talking to my mother:

"It's Tommy calling from T."

"How are you both?"

"Everything's fine."

"You don't sound very happy. Anything happened?"

"No, nothing. We saw the house."

"What condition is it in?"

"Not bad. Still very impressive."

"Did you get inside?"

"We got into the shops and into Frau Gisela's and the engineer's apartment."

"Those Nazis… are they still there?"

"No. There are other nice young people living there now."

"That's fine. Gisela used to be a friend of mine, but you already know that, and we're talking long distance."

"Don't worry about it."

"You're Sigmund's grandson! Where are you staying?"

"At the Hotel Krantz."

"Our old hotel. Are the rooms as neat as they used to be?"

"How would you know?" I ventured.

"Don't be cheeky to your Mama! Take care of yourselves. I dreamt you were being chased down the street as far as the bridge. Don't do anything foolish, and don't stay in T. longer than you have to. I know you don't like me giving you advice, but…"

"You can never resist it, Mama. How are you all? The kids and the grandchildren? We don't read the newspapers here, any troubles over there?"

"Don't you worry. We're all right. Kiss your wife for me. Women like to be pampered, you know. Your Papa's a wonderful husband, but he's very stingy about compliments, as if any kind word costs a fortune. Did I ever tell you this?"

"Many, many times."

"Be nice. Say 'Never!'"

"Never, ever."

"That's better. Tell your charming wife I'm knitting her a pullover. And take care."

Papa asked if we had already visited Frau Schtiasna, and posed a few questions about the upkeep of the house and the shops below, and about the tenants. However, since he suspected wire-tapping he contented himself with general answers and a promise that I'd tell him everything in detail once I got back home.

I paid for my call and sat down to watch television: a close soccer match between Rome and Milan. My wife, who seemed bored, said she was going up to our room to read a book. Almost as soon as she was out of the way the receptionist swiveled his armchair in my direction:

"I almost forgot to tell you, Frau Schtiasna was asking whether you had arrived."

"We'll be calling on her tomorrow."

"Good, good. But I have to ask you something." He seemed to be having difficulty getting it out.

"So ask!"

"I've heard that you were born..." He hesitated.

"It's written on the form I filled in here."

"True, true. I didn't notice it at first."

"So who told you?

"T. is a small town. As soon as you started snooping people picked up the phone and asked questions."

"People? What people?"

"You seem to be interrogating me like…"

"I'm sorry, please go on."

"People are worried about your intentions."

"I've no intentions."

"Beware the bear who guards his lair."

"Are you hinting at something?"

"You'd be better off not getting involved with them. Maybe you'll be cutting your visit short and going back to Prague?"

"Somebody tipped you to scare me off?"

"You do me wrong, sir."

"Sorry again. Forgive me. I'm staying here for three nights because we want to go to Poland to visit B."

"B.?"

He was blushing, trying to swallow back his phlegm and clutching his throat. He leaned toward me and spoke in a hoarse whisper, his lips brushing my ear:

"Who would the gentleman be looking for in B.?"

"My grandfather's grave: Zelig Biegeleisen."

There was a long silence, then (as if Joseph had finally decided to meet his brethren) he said in faltering Yiddish, "I grew up in B."

"So there are still Jews in T. after all."

"Swear to me you'll never tell a soul."

"I'm not the gossiping type."

"I believe you. Biegeleisen? I seem to recall that name. When did he die?"

"A year before the outbreak of the Second World War."

"Biegeleisen you said? Had a greengrocer's on Railway Street?"

"That's him!"

"Short fellow, broad-shouldered with a big beard?"

"That's my Grandpa! Tough guy, his father was a butcher."

"I remember looking at the store window of that greengrocers': piles of oranges, Jaffas they used to call them. I'd be dribbling just to taste one of them. I'd have given up my place in paradise just for one bite. We didn't have any money. Dad died in the plague when I was only seven. I'd almost got used to going to bed hungry, sucking my thumb. When Mama would come home with a loaf of bread we'd have a party. Then I'd see Rebbe Biegeleisen coming at me out of his store. I was sure he was going to kick me off the pavement, like a stray dog, but he beckoned to me with his finger, offering me a slice of orange. 'Take it, my boy. Taste the taste of the Land of Israel,' he said."

"Mama will be happy to know that you remember Grandpa Zelig. She used to be tiny, with two long braids."

"I only remember Rebbe Biegeleisen. He was a pious man. I thought he'll yell at me, tell me off, but instead he gave me a taste of the Holy Land."

"Where can I get a taxi around here to B.?"

"Not worth your while to go there. Those Polaks don't like Jews."

"Have you been there lately?"

"The last time I went to B. was on the fiftieth anniversary of my father's death. I wanted to visit his grave and recite *Shema Yisroel*. I don't remember Kaddish and I don't have a prayer book. Even if I had one, I wouldn't be able to read the Hebrew words. Now and then when my wife makes the sign of the cross and prays to Jesus, I whisper *Shema Yisroel*. I think He hears me."

"I am sure He does! Does your wife know?"

"Of course she does. She's a good woman. It was her parents who hid me."

"What does it look like now, the cemetery at B.?"

"What does it look like? It's an eyesore! Those Polaks stole the tombstones, then they bulldozed the whole area and built apartment blocks for the working class."

"So there's nothing there for me to look for."

"*A feig*," he said in Yiddish. "Nothing," he told me accompanied by a heavy Jewish sigh.

I waited a moment before going on.

"Why are you so afraid of people finding out you're Jewish?"

"What are you, a kid, asking questions like this. Listen? when I applied for a residence permit to live here in T., they were asking all kind of questions. You could only get a work permit for a job in a hotel if you had a clean record. So I said my mother and father were Poles, and I thought they bought it. But when I went to get my license, this guy took me into the other room and told me straight to my face that I was a liar and an imposter. Maybe my wife, who's an innocent woman, might have let something slip. So this guy says he couldn't give a damn if I'm a Jew cause they're not anti-Semites and they're relying on me to be grateful to the comrades who turn a blind eye. But I should be a good fellow and keep an eye on the guests, and on the boss, just so he shouldn't steal too much. I was supposed to hide away like a worm in a cabbage."

"Isn't it time to stop hiding?"

"How can I? What'd the neighbors say if they knew I was actually a Jew? How can I do that to my kids?" He was grabbing at my sleeve by now, spilling his guts. "I beg of you, don't get me involved in your affairs. All my family was wiped out in the Holocaust apart from a cousin of mine living somewhere abroad. I've got a new name. A new family. I've got children and grandchildren! Please leave me alone, you promised you would."

"Relax. I told you I'm not a squealer. Do you know the Schtiasna family?"

"They had a hard time under the Reds."

"What did they do?"

"Ask them yourself. They're no friends of mine."

LATER ON while talking to my wife I mentioned that our Jewish kinsman seemed to be pressing us to get out of town as soon as we could.

"I'm ready to pack our bags and catch the first train."

"But I'm eager to meet Frau Schtiasna."

"I hope she's not as pretty as that Anna!"

"She must be at least eighty years old."

"In that case we can get a good night's sleep."

I checked whether the door was locked and then went across to the window to gaze out at the starlit summer night in my slumber-wrapped hometown. There was a light winking here and there, maybe a student cramming for his exam, maybe an old man suffering from insomnia, perhaps a woman in labor? Down below in the street the overloaded cars were still wending their way toward the border checkpoint like refugees fleeing from siege.

*   *   *

THE NEXT DAY, on our way to the Schtiasna home, we passed through the main square, flanked by the town hall. Peasants and peddlers were standing by their stalls selling practically everything: farm produce, clothing, furniture, and household utensils, both new and used. I wandered along the benches searching in vain for a silver wine cup (with a Hebrew inscription) or a candelabrum, something which might have been taken away from our home so long ago.

Retirees were dragging themselves up the shallow steps leading to the towering town hall. With the changing regimes the various brass reliefs had been defaced, including that of the beloved President Masaryk. Once, when President Masaryk came to visit T., the presidential train was halted a kilometer before the station, where the mayor and a full-blown reception committee awaited him; the president stepped down from his luxury Pullman car to embrace the schoolchildren who lined the track with their white-red-and-blue flags, and walked with them on foot all the way to town. His plaques had been replaced by images of sturdy Stachanovite workers, which were also torn down after the Velvet Revolution. Now there was only an open pit and a few rusty iron frameworks awaiting a new statue "of the Playwright-President," or the long-awaited maker of the financial miracle.

IT WAS HERE that the local magistrate officiated over Mama and Papa's civil marriage ceremony in the presence of many local dignitaries. The Jewish religious ceremony was held at the Biegeleisen's home in B. I was informed by my sources (Mama) that Grandpa Sigmund only agreed to go to B. and rub shoulders with "those Polish Jews" on condition that the rabbi keep his sermon short. Before the marriage contract was signed Grandpa Sigmund had drawn Grandpa Zelig to one side and told him he was willing to forgo the dowry. Grandpa Zelig, who had his pride, rejected the offer:

"Hilde will bring with her exactly what her elder three sisters did."

"I don't need your money, Zelig. Just give Hilde that trunk of bedclothes she's embroidered so it won't be said I brought Walter a bankrupt bride."

"She'll get what's coming to her, even if we have to cancel the wedding!"

Grandpa Sigmund gave in: Walter would never have forgiven him, and besides, he had grown quite fond of little Hilde.

We stood for some time on the riverbank staring at the rancid waters with floating plastic bottles and foam from pollution of the nearby factories. On the opposite Polish bank we could see a barrier of coiled barbed-wire with a gap in the middle. From across this border the warm breeze bore snatches of conversation in Polish that rasped on my ears. In the tops of the maple trees that lined the stream, gray and black ravens were cawing.

We left the river for the park: mothers and baby-sitters gossiping, kids playing hide-and-seek, building sand-castles, swinging on the swings, swiveling the steering-wheels of abandoned cars and tooting, "Too-Tooo-Toooo!" An old lady was scattering breadcrumbs for the pigeons, mumbling to them. Then suddenly she laughed out loud. Upon seeing us, she demanded, "Why aren't you laughing too?"

When I didn't respond she waved a bony finger at me like the Wicked Witch in Hansel and Gretel.

"If you don't laugh I'll banish you from my garden!"

I went back to strolling through the park, trying to recall that same Tommy who used to play here with Grandpa, when all of a sudden, Frau Schtiasna's little daughter leaped out at me from behind the shrubbery, the one who used to have a doll whose eyes would open and close. What was her name? Zelma? No. She was wearing a checkered dress with a lace collar, long white stockings, and gleaming black patent-leather shoes.

"Be careful not to get dirty!" her nanny would yell at her. "Have a nice quiet game with Tommy."

But Zelma (that couldn't have been her name) was more interested in her doll: dressing her, undressing her, laying her down to sleep, whispering secrets in her ear that I was not privy to hear. Once when I was chasing her, she let me catch her and then, as we stood breathlessly facing each other, she flashed me a brazen three-year old glance and demanded, "Give me a kiss, the way Papa kisses Luisa the cook."

I was confused. I didn't know what to do. She was standing on tiptoe offering me her lips. Being an obedient child, I did what she asked and then bolted.

"Coward!" she screamed after me. I avoided her for a couple of days, scared to death that she might want me to kiss her again. But she didn't give up, until one day she caught me and told me I was a fool and a baby, and that if I didn't want her, she'd find another bridegroom! I remember closing my eyes and hoping it would all be over soon, but she (what the hell was the name of my first love?) said that it's not worth anything with the eyes closed. That's how it started. After a few such kisses (during which she would act out the part of the cook, screaming "Leave me alone! Take your hands off my ass!") I got used to the rules of the game and began to enjoy it. Until one day Nanny Hela heard her screaming and rushed over to where we were and caught us in the heat of the act. Hela was shocked: "That's no way for a well-brought-up boy to behave!"

Hela warned me that if I ever molested that innocent girl again she'd tell my parents about what a little monster they were bringing up.

Meanwhile, little what's-her-name stood off to one side, wiping away a tear and sticking out her tongue at me.

I dragged my wife into a sudden, passionate embrace: "Give me a kiss, my love."

"What's come over you? That old woman there, the baby-sitters, they're all looking at us."

"Let them look. Do you see a sign that reads 'No kissing in the park'?

\*    \*    \*

FRAU SCHTIASNA OPENED HER DOOR with a welcoming smile while mumbling, "You must be Tommy!" She was dressed in a flowered house dress missing two buttons. Her dyed red hair was in disarray, and she offered a wrinkled, powdered cheek for a kiss.

"What a pleasant surprise! Just give me a few minutes to make myself look respectable."

She pranced off into another room with that lightweight step that only heavy people seem to manage. I looked around at the armchairs, at the mahogany cupboard, at the oil-paintings in their laurel-wreathed frames, at the tapestry she had once stitched in her youth, and realized that in fact, this was not so different from my own parents' living room. Just a little overcrowded, as if furniture from three other rooms had been stuffed in.

Frau Schtiasna returned dressed in a brown skirt and a yellow linen blouse, her damp hair combed with a part on the right. She was bearing a tray with crystal goblets and a crimson-filled decanter along with a plate of cookies.

"Such a pity Ernst isn't at home. I told him you might be calling, but he wasn't ready to give up his card game and gossip in the old-folks' club. 'What have you got to chat about so much?' I ask him. 'Why Czechs and Slovaks can't get along?'"

"So tell me about yourselves. How is Walter? Still tall and handsome? And what about Hilde? A real doughnut she used to be, just inviting a nip!"

I presented Frau Schtiasna with a couple of pairs of socks that Mama had knitted, a can of Israeli instant coffee, and a brooch made by a Jerusalem silversmith. I told her that my aging parents lived together close to the Lebanese border in comparative tranquility, that they swim in the pool, stroll along the beach, play bridge (at which Mama is better), and derive great joy from their grandchildren and great-grandchildren. I reassured her that my father was still tall and handsome and still dressed like a gentleman, that Mama writes books and knits pullovers for developmentally delayed children and is still proud of her figure. What I didn't tell her was that Papa walks stooped over, leaning on a stick, and is always visiting the doctor (whether he has to or not.), or that Mama, ever since Bergen-Belsen, suffers from nightmares and diarrhea.

Frau Schtiasna poured us some Vishniak, spilling a few drops on the lace tablecloth. We all raised our glasses in a toast.

Our hostess was eager to hear more and more, but when I begged her to recall some memories of my earlier family life in T., she went into a trance that threw me off balance.

"I was also in love with Walter, just don't tell your mother about it. I had two or three other admirers, who I used to twist around my little finger. This one, with the ugly arthritis. But really I was mad about your father. He was so tall, so polite, so honest. When we would arrange to meet on the riverbank, he'd be there fifteen minutes early and with a gift – a kerchief or a ribbon for my hair. I was always late.

"He knew how to bow to you, how to invite you to dance, and he never stepped on your toes. True, he wasn't a tennis player like Ivan Lendel or Korda, but he never lost his temper, never threw down his racquet when he lost. He was a gentle creature and had other qualities that I won't go into now.

"It was Walter himself who told me he was going to be engaged to Hilde and asked me to forgive him. He promised always to remember me.

"'Don't be a fool,' I comforted him, 'I've forgotten about you already,' Why don't you try the cookies. Tommy?

"I made friends with your Grandma Valli, but I couldn't stand your Grandpa Sigmund. He had too much self-confidence and was too clever for me. My girlfriends used to call Valli "the Iceberg." They used to say that if she ever smiled, she'd melt. We were pretty nasty in those days about everybody. One time I came to the store looking for a crocodile-leather belt for my father. We could always find nice presents at your place. When I went in I saw Valli sitting next to the cash register, and she appeared to be weeping. When she noticed me she straightened up.

"'What can we offer you, miss?'

"'Anything wrong, madam?' I dared to ask.

"'Just a sharp pain, somewhere here, below the heart.'

"'Should I call the doctor?'

"'It's all right. I sent Walter upstairs to get some codeine.'

"'Should I stay here with you?'

"'If you wish. Tell me, weren't you once my son's girlfriend?'

"'Yes, I was.'

"'But he chose another.' There was something almost cruel about the way she said it. 'No, no, I've no complaints about my daughter-in-law; she's a loving and loyal wife. But I don't think she likes me all that much, if you know what I mean.'

"'Maybe you're mistaken, Madame? I know Hilde very well. She always speaks kindly about you.'

"'Really?!'

"A smile at last. The iceberg must be melting, I said to myself. From then on I was a regular visitor, telling the old lady about everything that was going on with the 'youngsters.' Valli was always asking about Hilde. I became her eyes and her ears. But there was no real gossip. She adored your Papa and never looked at another man. Even when Walter went abroad to Palestine, she acted as if he could see from there whoever she was going out with! I wasn't all that faithful, may God and Ernst forgive me.

"Valli was very fond of you, even if she didn't hug and kiss you. She loathed the way everyone petted you and gave you gifts, particularly Sigmund. He once bought you a pony, didn't he? Because you liked the ponies you'd see in the circus.

"'Tommy doesn't have to get everything he wants!' she used to say. 'God doesn't hand out only sweets and cream-puffs!'

"She wanted Sigmund to take the pony back to the circus, but he didn't agree. It was only when the pony started filling up the backyard with droppings and kept neighing at siesta time that your grandfather got rid of it.

"Your grandmother came from a large family in the country. The older children would look after the youngsters, and youngsters would get the older ones' hand-me-downs. Valli, who was in the middle, had never had a new dress until she was grown up. She once told me she used to torment her elder sister by saying to her. 'Eat lots of yeast and grow quicker, I want that dress of yours!' Once, years before your Mama came into the family, Sigmund came back from one of his buying trips to Vienna, and he brought Valli this huge straw hat decorated with a velvet ribbon and a bunch of grapes. Your grandmother said, 'Thanks,' and wouldn't even try it on when he begged her to.

"'I'll look ridiculous with that fruit salad on my head. I don't want the ladies turning up their noses and laughing behind my back.'

"Sigmund put the hat back in its box without a word, and when the mayor's wife was in the shop the next day, he sold it to her. Your grandmother nearly had a fit."

I moved back to the present. "What's your daughter doing nowadays?" I asked.

"Bertha? I was waiting for you to ask. I remember the nanny once telling me…Do you want your wife to hear about this?"

"Bertha, that was her name?"

"Have you forgotten?"

"No, of course not. Tell us about her. But you should know, it was Bertha who started with the kisses."

"That's what all men say!" Frau Schtiasna took a deep breath. "It hasn't been at all rosy for Bertha, for all of us." Tears began running down her cheeks carving damp furrows in the mask of face powder.

"We used to be people of property, capitalists like your grandfather. My father had a china factory that employed hundreds of workers. We had a big house up on the hill with cherry trees in the garden. The communists took over the factory and the house and put my father and Ernst to work in the kilns. 'Sweat a bit' they said, 'like the proletariat, and learn to make an honest living for a change.'

"Father collapsed and died within the year. Ernst went on firing that kiln until he retired on his pension. I, who was once a lady, worked for thirty years as a cashier at the supermarket, getting home with blisters on my feet. But I was able to get a few cans of food, some rolls of toilet paper, and a bit of meat here and there and hide it under the party newspaper in my basket. They'd sell that stuff on the cheap to the workers. At the cash desk you'd hear everything that was going on in town: who was on the up-and-up, whose wife was worth sucking up to, and who was on the way down. I don't regret a single moment of it."

"You were going to tell us about Bertha."

"Don't push me, Tommy. It's not so easy for me.

"When we wanted to register Bertha for high school the headmistress told us it had been 'decided' that Bertha should learn a trade.

"Ernst exploded. 'But she wants to matriculate and study medicine!'

"'There are enough of you educated rich folks,' the headmistress said. 'It's time to give a chance to the peasants and the workers.'

"'And the Party hacks!' I couldn't contain myself.

"'Watch your tongue, Comrade Schtiasna. I've no wish to cause you any trouble. Bertha's a bright girl and a good pupil, pity she isn't the daughter of a miner or a laborer.'

"'But I and my father...'

"'You're all right now, Comrade Schtiasna, but the Revolution has a long memory. It's all on record, just exactly who lived in mansions gorging themselves on roast duck while the workers starved and shivered in hovels with leaking roofs.'

"'So what do you suggest, Comrade Headmistress?' I asked her.

"'Write a letter to the Pedagogic Committee. It'll be debated in our next meeting. I'll do my best to persuade the comrades, but it isn't only up to me.'

"In the end they sent Bertha to learn sewing, and then to some workshop where they made uniforms for the army. They ruined the poor girl; it was like a nail in the heart. Bertha got married. That didn't work, so she got divorced and then got married again. She's got two sweet children, but she's very unhappy."

"And drinking?"

"How did you know that, Tommy?"

"Yesterday I dropped in on the tavern to ask my way to the hotel..."

"And Bertha tried to scrounge a drink off you?"

"I didn't know it was your Bertha."

"Her husband's a good fellow, but after all, how much can he take?

"We've tried everything we know."

After wiping her eyes and blowing her nose, Frau Schtiasna's mood suddenly changed.

"Now let's talk about something more cheerful, Annushka, Bertha's eldest is, a beauty, just like her mother used to be. Well, when she turned eighteen we were afraid they wouldn't let us register her for university. That was when the students in Prague were out in Vaclav Square shouting slogans, lighting candles, rattling key chains, and throwing Hussak out on his ear – when things began to move a bit. Mind you we haven't got our property back yet, that takes time. However, on the application form for the university they've cancelled those registrations of 'Original Social Status,' which was why they did the dirt to our Havel. Only this week we were informed that Annushka has been accepted by the Faculty of Medicine in O. What do you say to this?"

"That calls for a celebration! Maybe this'll..."

"Every night I pray for Bertha to stop drinking. So instead of a glass of Vishniak, perhaps we'll all just embrace for Dr. Annushka's sake? Don't be shy, my Lady. We're all like one family."

Frau Schtiasna pulled me into her ample embrace, leaving face powder and lipstick all over my cheeks. My wife, too, didn't escape. When we were free again I asked Frau Schtiasna about our tenants.

"That woman with the limp, who rents your big shop, has got a bed hidden behind the curtain. What for, I ask you?"

"She told me that's where she takes a rest when there aren't any customers."

"I don't call that 'taking a rest,' and believe me, I know what I'm talking about. Anyway, what business is it of mine? Good luck to her! Tell me, Tommy, what do men find so attractive in cripples?"

"Maybe they pity them," I suggested.

"You're as naive as your father was!"

"Who rents Mama's shop?"

"New people. I don't know them. I don't know everybody in T."

"And the woman in Grandpa's apartment?"

"That communist cow? She used to be on the Health Committee, used to drive the patients crazy before handing out a permit for the rest home.

"'What are you so stingy about?' I used to ask her. 'Does the place belong to your father?'

"'Shut up, you bourgeois!' she'd snarl. 'Otherwise...'

"'What more can you do to us? Give me that permit for Ernst, I've got to get back to the supermarket.'

"'What've you got today?'

"'Smoked salmon from Finland, I lied to her, and made off with the permit."

"Do you know the mother of the twins?" asked my wife.

"You've met Anna? Looks like Steffi Graff. Such legs, such a figure! And such charming little kids. Anna's father used to be one of those loyal communists who only had to be told what to think and what to do and then he'd simply think it and do it. After the Prague Spring he woke up and saw what was what. He couldn't handle it and put a bullet through his head. You can imagine...no you can't, what a shock it was for Anna and her mother. One week later she handed back her Communist Youth Movement uniform and became a dissident. Anna was active in a cell that often met in our home. Ernst had this old typewriter on which he used to hack out pamphlets. Anna actually met Jan for the first time in our house. I could see at once they were stuck on each other. I remember saying to Ernst, 'Look at the lovebirds.' 'You and your romantic ideas,' he scoffed me. But who was right?" She gave a slight chuckle before continuing.

"Not much later Anna told me that Jan had asked her out to a concert at A. In those days tickets to concerts and the theater only cost a few crowns."

As Frau Schtiasna paused for a brief moment, I managed to edge in a question.

"Is Frau Gisela still alive?"

"Alive and kicking, and she's got a son. Not from that Nazi Wolfgang either! He always blamed her for their not having pure-blooded Aryan children, until the Russians came and took Wolfgang away to Siberia. They wanted to deport Gisela along with all the other Germans who were kicked out of the Sudetenland, but she was lucky enough to have this friend, a dentist who promised to marry her, if it turned out that Wolfgang decided to settle in Siberia or if he froze to death. In the meantime the dentist got her pregnant and then married the daughter of some general, or maybe he was only a major. There's men for you! Gisela, who always was a practical creature, rented a room, studied hairdressing, got herself a job at the Salon Moldava, and brought the child up by herself. She'd do me a set and a rinse at half price until she retired on her pension and returned to her family in Heidelberg. What was I saying when you interrupted? I don't think so quickly these days."

IT WAS PLEASANT CHATTING with Frau Schtiasna, nibbling at her singed poppy seed cakes, listening to all the gossip, and feeling just a tiny bit at home, but I had already made up my mind to leave T. on the noon train.

"Come again!" Frau Schtiasna implored. "Bring Walter and Hilde. I want to see them once again before… And thank them for the letter and the dollars. They really shouldn't have. Such a pity you didn't meet Ernst, but nothing can drag him away from his cards and his politics. As for Bertha, well you've already seen her."

\* \* \*

WHEN WE INFORMED the receptionist that we were leaving T. he mumbled a blessing in Yiddish. Checking the accounts, he announced that since he had not yet put the money in the bank, he could refund us for two nights.

"You ought to get a move on. The 12:58 train only stops for two minutes."

The sign had been removed from the door of the elevator, so we squeezed inside and groaned and rattled our way up.

"Going down, I'll take the stairs," my wife commented.

OUR PAJAMAS WERE as we had left them, the remnants of last night's food were still in the trashcan. But the open suitcase, the smell of tobacco, and the cigarette butts in the ashtray revealed that someone had gone through our things without bothering to cover his tracks.

"Check if anything is missing."

"In a moment, Tommy. You've got the money and the passports in your kangaroo-pouch?"

"Yes."

"It all looks all right, except that nauseating smell. Now if you'll excuse me I've got to –"

"Me too. You go first."

When she emerged from the bathroom, my wife whispered, "If my ears aren't playing tricks on me, there's someone in the next room."

"Must be the regular guest. Why are you whispering?"

"I don't know. Now it's your turn. I'm going to pack."

I yanked on the piece of rope and listened to the triumphant roar of waters cascade from the tank into the bowl. The sound seemed to echo throughout the entire empty floor, then silence. With my ear to the bathroom wall I could hear the scrape of a chair, a key in the lock, and a door opening. After a moment there was a soft knock on our door. Opening it I was confronted by a wizened-looking seventy-year-old man with a mane of white hair and a small scar on his nose. He was wearing a blue suit with a red bow tie, and was examining us through watery blue eyes. He asked in German if he might come in.

"If you have a search warrant," I replied.

"Pardon?"

"Somebody's been going through our luggage."

"Has anything been taken?"

"Doesn't look like it. Please come in."

"Doktor Herman Freulich, lawyer," the man introduced himself.

With a small, stiff bow and a kiss on my wife's hand, he seated himself in the only chair in the room. I told him our names.

"Delighted to make your acquaintance. The receptionist told me that the lady and gentleman are from Israel."

"From Jerusalem."

"*Ja, ja.* Jerusalem." He seemed slightly ill at ease. Looking at me he said, "I see you staring at the scar on my nose. Make no mistake, I am not of your people, but I have suffered very much for having a hooked nose. My classmates used to call me Judas. The Gestapo snatched me off the street for not wearing the yellow star. I showed them my papers, told them I was a law student, but they claimed they could see exactly what I was and dragged me down to headquarters. I pleaded with them to call my parents and gave them the address. They jeered at me that my parents' turn would come soon enough and that they had never seen such a snotty little cockroach such as me. They beat me with rubber truncheons and broke my ribs and my nose. I was ready to sign a declaration that

I (who else?) had crucified Jesus, that my proper name was Albert Einstein, or even Herman Goering, whatever, just so long as they would stop beating me and let me close my eyes. Eventually, as I was lying on the floor, certain this was the end, I asked for a priest. The priest came, kneeled over me, wrung his hands, made the sign of the cross, and swore to God that he personally had baptized me. They kicked me out of there with a warning not to go around showing my Jewish nose. I went in there a young man with jet-black hair. When I crawled out, it was all white."

I waited a moment and then asked, "By any chance did you hear anybody enter our room?"

"Heard nothing, saw nothing."

"Hostile witness," I muttered to my wife in Hebrew.

"Perhaps it was the maid?"

"Look at the beds. You're a lawyer, aren't you?"

"A lawyer for the province," he said with a slight smirk. "You say nothing was stolen?"

"Not as far as we can tell," my wife responded.

"So there are no complaints."

"Do you still go around searching foreigners' luggage and placing hidden microphones? In what era do you think you're living?"

"I have lived under so many regimes that I find it difficult to answer."

"Whoever was here smokes cheap cigarettes and deliberately left a stub in the ashtray."

"Amateur!"

"I said deliberately... intentionally."

"Intentions are difficult things to prove."

"Perhaps it's meant to be some kind of warning?"

"Perhaps."

"You haven't answered my husband's question."

"I've answered it according to the evidence at my disposal. And now, madam, sir, after satisfying my curiosity, I must return to my room and to my own misfortunes."

I wasn't going to let him off that easy.

"May I ask you for a professional opinion?"

"Concerning what?"

"You've served as a lawyer under the communist regime?"

"*Natuerlich.* Forty years of loyal service as a defense lawyer. I even won an acquittal here and there. But even when I lost, my clients were satisfied because I used to tell those bastards exactly what the people wanted them to hear. The judges threatened to revoke my license, but somewhere up in the upper echelons somebody hinted that I should be left alone to bark as I saw fit. I also represented the Schtiasna family, with whom I understand you are acquainted, in the matter of their factory. I lost, appealed the case, and lost again. The second time I didn't ask for a fee. Don't imagine I was sufficiently naive to believe in such a Kafkaesque judicial system. After the Slansky trial I knew we were all of us convicted. So was I hypocritical? Corrupt? No, not Herr Doktor Herman Freulich! True, there were deals with those gentlemen who drafted the verdicts; my late mother used to say that if you're dealing with horse traders you've got to be stubborn like a mule. But I never sold my soul for the fattened calf. I was never a party member. I never signed manifestos. Somebody had to act the role of counsel for the defense, and I was always blessed with a certain theatrical talent. There were, of course, some bleeding hearts who accused me of collaborating with the secret police, but the investigation committee cleared my name and restored my rights."

"How should we go about recovering our property?"

"You're asking me?"

"Who else? What steps would you take, supposing you were representing us?"

The Herr Doktor clutched his ribcage and let out a long and painful sigh.

"But I represent the residents in that building. I was summoned here when it became known you were nosing around the stores, attempting to get into their homes."

"That is my father's and grandfather's house. We have the papers to prove it!"

"Indeed?" The watery eyes seemed to be lighting up.

"Is that what you were looking for?"

"The gentleman does me a grave injustice by making such an accusation."

In spite of my good manners I was tempted to grab the old boy and shake him until his teeth rattled. Somehow sensing this, the lawyer began to edge toward the door, nevertheless voicing an objection.

"You Israelis have become such aggressive people! The law of this land determines the penalty for grave bodily assault as five years in jail. However I have no wish to cause you any difficulties; let us part as civilized people. It has been a great pleasure to make your acquaintance."

And he was out through the door, swift as a lizard.

*　　*　　*

WE DRAGGED OUR SUITCASE and hand baggage down to the desk. The receptionist returned our dollars and I gave him a tip.

"You'll forgive my presumption, but I have a great favor to ask."

"Which is?"

"Could you take a note from me, a supplication to slip between the stones of the Western Wall?"

"Gladly. No harm can befall the emissaries of good."

"I'm sorry, I didn't understand that bit."

"It's an ancient Jewish proverb."

"Ah, yes, I forgot all I had studied as a kid. Let me help you with your suitcase."

"There's no need, we can manage."

"Permit me all the same. We must hurry; the train is approaching the station."

We rushed downstairs along the murky corridor and through the abandoned dining room. As we frantically crossed the street, we could hear the loudspeaker announcements, the slamming of carriage doors, and the shrill blast of the station manager's whistle. By the time we reached the platform the engine was already emitting puffs of white smoke and the train was on its way.

"The next train is at 4:35." He tried to break the news to us gently. "Come back to the hotel and rest. I'll try to arrange for some food."

"Thank you. We'd prefer to wait here at the station."

"Then we must part. I have to get back to work."

We stood on the platform, embarrassed and fatigued, watching the train speed ahead like an arrowhead into the far distance. The all-too-efficient station manager, and a broad woman in a grey smock, who was sweeping the platform with a birch broom, shrugged their shoulders. We sat on one of the wooden benches gazing at each other like two accused people being punished for a crime they had never committed.

"I hope we don't have to stay in T. forever," my wife said.

"Don't tempt the devil. Can you see the woman peering out at us from the mouth of the passenger tunnel?"

"Yes, I noticed her."

We were approached by an old woman with a kerchief around her head who was carrying a straw basket.

"Herr and Frau H.?" she addressed us in old-fashioned German.

"Yes?"

"You missed your train, never mind, there'll be another one at four thirty-five."

"May I inquire as to your name?"

"Yermilla. I used to work in the patisserie opposite your grandfather's house. Your mother and father used to come in for cakes and cocoa with whipped cream. I remember Nanny Hela wheeling the little gentleman in his carriage, and the little dog wagging his tail and barking at anyone who dared get near you. I never even dared to try. When I heard from Frau Schtiasna...Maybe I shouldn't have mentioned it. Anyway, when I heard that you and your wife were leaving on the midday train I said to myself, 'Yermilla, go and say hello to Herr Tommy!' Luckily I had some butter cake in the storeroom. I learned how to make it at the patisserie. I also had a can of real coffee. So I filled up a thermos for you, and I've been waiting down in the tunnel trying to gather up the courage to come and say hello. So here I am, have some coffee and cakes. I can give the lady the recipe?"

"That's very, very kind of you, Frau Yermilla!" we both said.

We sipped the strong coffee and nibbled at the crisp, sweet cake. My wife sifted through her handbag and finally produced a miniature camel caravan, which she offered to our benefactress:

"These are made of olivewood, from Bethlehem."

"From the birthplace of our Savior?"

"Yes, from there."

"Bless you both."

Yermilla's lips were trembling as she clutched the tiny camels to her chest.

All of a sudden the lawyer appeared on the platform.

"You haven't gone yet?"

"Seems like you'll have to apply for an eviction order."

"The gentleman is extremely offensive."

"Get away, you snake!" Yermilla yelled at him.

"Watch your tongue, you old fool! I came to be of assistance to these people. Sir, Madame, please believe I only have your best interests at heart."

Not finding this worthy of any reaction, I went on drinking my coffee as Herr Doktor Freulich vanished into the station manager's office.

"Silly old goat," Yermilla grumbled.

At 4:30 I stepped down off the platform and applied an ear to the rusted, silent rails. A moment later the station manager and Dr. Freulich emerged to inform us that the 4:35 wouldn't be arriving today.

"That's a bit too much!" exclaimed my wife, by now quite agitated.

"What happened?" I inquired as calmly as I could.

"There's been a crash, the lines are blocked."

"Are there injuries?"

"We don't know yet."

"When's the next train?"

"The 7:30 doesn't stop at T. Anyhow, they seem to be having problems with the rescue teams. Maybe you can take the night train at 02:10, or at the very worst, the 12:58 tomorrow, if you are on time."

The station manager retired into his office. The lawyer was still hanging around watching us, but apparently wary of Yermilla, he kept his distance.

"I'd be happy to have you stay with me," offered Yermilla. "It's only two and a half rooms, and my grandson and his wife, three kids and the dog live with me, but we can surely find you both a corner."

"I don't know how to thank you, but really, we can't accept."

"Why ever not? We could have a little party! It's been years since we had classy guests like you."

"Please forgive us, but we are expected in Vienna," my wife responded. "I'm not staying here tonight," she said to me in Hebrew.

"You could have our beds." Yermilla was as insistent as a young girl with a reluctant boyfriend.

"Next time," I quickly promised.

"In that case, I'll leave the thermos with you."

Yermilla gave me a brief, bone-crushing handshake, nodded a cool farewell to my wife, and gathering her flowing skirts about her, vanished swiftly into the gloom of the passenger tunnel.

Once he felt he was out of danger, the lawyer approached us, speaking rapidly. "I have ordered a rental car from K. The driver will take you as far as Z., there you can catch the train to Vienna. We agreed on a price of fifteen dollars. If you think that's too much, give him ten and I will make up the difference."

"Charging it on expenses?"

"I have already told you, I am only eager to be of assistance."

"Are you expecting an apology of some sort?"

"In my experience, any client who is given free advice turns out to be ungrateful. Come, the driver is waiting."

"Tell him to stop off at our place. I want to say goodbye."

"Very well, but I beg you – no provocations. I have enough problems as it is."

WE DRAGGED our luggage after him to the awaiting black Skoda. The lawyer was giving instructions to the driver, who lit a cigarette and turned the ignition.

"Excuse me," I tried in German, "but your smoking bothers us. If you can manage without a cigarette until we get to Z., I will give you a pack of American cigarettes when we arrive."

The driver glowered at me, but nevertheless stubbed out the cigarette.

"You are spoiled by luxury," sneered Herr Doktor. "Take care!"

The driver pulled up opposite our house, and I heaved myself out of the cramped vehicle to stand gazing at the shops, their signs, the spacious entryway, the windows, the little veranda with its window boxes full of petunias, and the dormer window of the attic. My wife was curled up in the back seat watching me anxiously, uncertain whether to get out and join me or simply leave me to myself. Eventually she got out of the car to stand beside me, take my hand in hers, and not say a word. The driver took off his peaked hat and regarded us as a couple in mourning taking our leave from a grave. I gave him a sign that he could have a cigarette. He nodded his gratitude, slipped out of the car, and stood blowing perfect smoke rings up towards a cloudy sky.

ON THE FIRST of September 1939, Mama took a man's raincoat from the coat rack in the big shop, emptied the till, locked the door, and went up to the apartment above the shop. She packed a small knapsack (she and Papa had used it once on their treks through the mountains), and took a last glance around the richly furnished rooms still filled with her possessions and mementos. On a sudden impulse, she ripped the tapestry from its frame, the tapestry that she had labored on some ten years, and stuffed it into the knapsack. Then she left, slamming the oak door behind her. Out on the street she swore she would not look back, but when she was approaching the bridge, she faltered, and like Lot's wife threw a glance over her shoulder at the burning Sodom.

Just as we were about to go I noticed a woman I seemed to recognize. After a moment of hesitation I waved to her.

My wife watched me, puzzled, but did not ask questions.

The woman was talking to an elderly gentleman, who seemed to be ogling at her figure and negotiating a price. The woman said something and then turned away. A moment later they seemed to have struck a bargain and vanished arm-in-arm into the stairwell of our home.

"Do you know her?" I asked the driver.

He chuckled a little coarsely, "Sure I know her. Everyone knows Bertha!"

*   *   *

THE TRAIN FROM Z. to Vienna did, in fact, have a dining car, but we made do with some of Yermilla's by-now tepid coffee.

The train cut across pine forests, past holiday chalets, pasture land and lakes that are home to ducks and moorhens. In the distance one could glimpse the mountain peaks.

A pink-cheeked youthful conductor checked our tickets and asked (in English), if we were interested in buying Austrian currency.

"Not this time." I handed him a last pack of leftover American cigarettes. "Maybe you know a conductor we met on our trip to T.?" I inquired.

"His name?"

"I don't know his name," I explained. "He's older than you, wears glasses, is heavily built with a broad forehead. Unmarried and interested in archeology?"

"I'm afraid I don't know anyone like that."

"Is there another conductor apart from you on the train?"

"Jaroslav. He's mad about butterflies. I ask you, a family man who runs around the fields waving a net on a pole? When he catches them he stabs them in the back with a pin. He showed me his collection once, and I told him straight to his face, 'You'd be better off collecting stamps.' An archeologist? At school we were taught to look forward, to concentrate on the future!"

It was slowly getting dark. My exhausted wife was napping, leaning her curly head on my shoulder. She seemed to be having a pleasant dream because she was smiling in her sleep. I looked out at the darkening fields, listening to the monotonous rhythm of the wheels on the tracks, and it seemed to me that I was finally freed of T., just as when the doctor (Grandpa didn't trust midwives) severed the umbilical cord and separated me from my mother.

I also felt that the farther I traveled from T., the closer I was getting to Jerusalem.

I was well aware that at the old, neglected, end-of-the-line railway station in Jerusalem, which dates to the days of the Turks, there would be no Fire Brigade Band to welcome me. But who needs a band when he returns, like Odysseus, to Ithaca?

*   *   *

HILDE HUPPERT (nee Bigeleisen) was born in 1910 in Bielsko, Poland, to a religious Jewish family. Though a bright pupil, she was only permitted to finish elementary school, and was trained as a seamstress. After her marriage to Walter, the son of a well-to-do Jewish merchant family in Tesine, Czechoslovakia, she sold hats at the family shop. During the Holocaust, she was hidden with her son, Tommy, in a Polish village, was later arrested and sent to a ghetto, and then to Bergen-Belsen concentration camp. While her husband waited for them in Palestine, she bravely struggled to keep her son and herself alive, and with the help of Palestinian immigration certificates that Walter sent her, they survived. Hilde was appointed to head a group of 500 orphans, who were being sent from the camps to Palestine by the American Military authorities and the "Joint" in July 1945. Arriving at Haifa, where Walter was awaiting their arrival, Hilde wrote her memoirs in German. Her moving chronicle was edited by the famous writer Arnold Zweig, and published in Czechoslovakia and East Germany. The Hebrew version, translated by her son, Tommy, was published only in 1977. *Hand in Hand with Tommy* was also published in Dutch and Arabic. In Palestine Hilde gave birth to a second son, Shlomo. She worked in the family's small handbag shop, on the main street in Haifa, and wrote occasionally. Her novel *Doctor Veronika*, was published in Dutch, Hebrew and Polish. At ninety-three, she is writing a new novel, at the retirement home in Regba, in the north of Israel, where she now resides. Every day Hilde remembers her relatives, who were murdered by the Nazis. She is very proud of her large family, all of whom are living in Israel, including six great-grandchildren.

SHMUEL THOMAS HUPPERT (Tommy) was born in 1936 in Czechoslovakia. Throughout the war years, he remained with his mother – a very unusual situation for a child to have stayed with a parent – and struggled for survival. He immigrated to Palestine in 1945. After his army service, he studied Hebrew and English Literature at the Hebrew University, Jerusalem. Huppert wrote his Ph.D. thesis on "Exile and Redemption in the Poetry of Uri Zvi Greenberg," in 1977. He published a novel, *Beautiful Jews*, two collections of stories, five books for children and youngsters, radio-plays and literary articles. Recently he finished a new novel entitled *Conversations and Silences with Abu-Said*. He is currently researching the works of Imre Kertesz. Huppert received the Ka. Tzetnik Prize for his collection of stories, *Grandpa Hovers like a Heron*. He was senior editor and head of the literary programs for Israeli Radio, "Kol-Israel," from 1965 to 2001. Through the course of his career, he interviewed many eminent Israeli and international writers, including Paul Celan, Primo Levi, Elie Wiesel, Imre Kertesz, Bernard Malamud, Graham Greene, Heinrich Böll, Ziegfried Lenz, Wolf Biermann, Don DeLillo, Andre Brink, Nadine Gordimer and others. Dr. S.T. Huppert lectures in Hebrew, English and German. He lives with his family in Jerusalem.